Jesus Laughing

*"Whoever does the will of God is my brother,
and my sister, and my mother."* Jesus Mark 3:35

Christians
*"Truly, I say unto you, as you did it to one of the least of
these my brothers, you did it to me."*

Matthew 25:40

Jews
*"And what does the Lord require of you but to do justice,
and to love kindness and to walk humbly with your God."*

Micah 6:8

Humanitarians
"It is not an answer to insert into the life of an apprehended
offender an inspirational personality (mentor), it is THE
answer."

Judge W. W. Nuernberger of
Lincoln, Nebraska and many other judges

JESUS, VOLUNTEERS AND OUR CITY MISDEMEANOR COURTS

WHEN CHRISTIANS, JEWS AND HUMANITARIAN VOLUNTEERS SHARE CHRIST-LIKE LOVE WITH OFFENDERS, CITY COURTS ARE HAVENS OF HOPE AND HELP AND PREVENT MANY FELONIES

KEITH J. LEENHOUTS

Judge, Royal Oak, Michigan City Court, retired and Director of Court Volunteer Mentoring and Supporting Professional Volunteers National Dissemination Organizations, 1959 – 2006

XULON
PRESS

Jesus, Volunteers And Our City Misdemeanor Courts
by Keith J. Leenhouts, Retired Judge

Printed in the United States of America

ISBN 1-59781-973-5

Library of Congress Library Number: 73-15435

www.xulonpress.com

Keith J. Leenhouts, Retired Judge
jimleenhouts@cityanimation.com

DEDICATION

This book is dedicated to the some 7 million volunteers who, from 1959 to 2006, have made mission focused courts a <u>Haven of Hope and Help</u> and not a symbol of suffering and sadness in the life and minds of millions of defendants.

Their mission has been to bring the love and discipline of Jesus to apprehended offenders early in a life of crime by sharing their lives and values. Most of these volunteers base their lives and love on Jesus as their Lord and Savior. Some bring a Christ-like love and discipline based upon other religious and secular values and beliefs.

We thank God for all of these volunteers and humbly dedicate this book to their love for the apprehended offender. By their efforts, they have diverted many young misdemeanants from a life of crime and have helped us better meet the challenge of crime in and to a free society.

Jesus, when His time on earth came to an end, left the task of establishing his kingdom to His disciples. They changed the world.

When the court seeks to bring the love of Jesus to the defendant, it gives the task to Christians and those living lives which reflect the love and discipline of Jesus.

They changed the lives of many defendants.

The United States now incarcerates a greater percentage of its citizens than any other comparable democracy in the world. Is it possible that we would be approaching the very dubious distinction of putting twice as many of our citizens in jail and prison than any other similar nation if it were not for the volunteers in misdemeanor and juvenile courts? Surveys and research so indicate.

In 1987 a survey was conducted by Volunteers in Probation, Inc., with the assistance of the U.S. Census Bureau. It identified 5,657,000 volunteers active in courts nationwide, 1959 – 1987. A very conservative estimate in 2006 would be some seven million, 1959 – 2006. These volunteers were very effective. They greatly reduced repeat misdemeanor convictions by over 90%. Since some 70% of all felonies are committed by those who have been <u>first</u> convicted of a misdemeanor, many felonies have been prevented by these volunteers. See index for details on the National Institutes of Health – Royal Oak City Research. Thank God for the some seven million volunteers.

A current excellent bestselling book urges us to live purpose-driven lives. We now recognize a small army of some 7 million citizen volunteers who have, and are doing, just that! By focusing on their mission to make our misdemeanor (usually city) courts <u>Havens of Hope and Help</u>, they have brought the love of Jesus to countless apprehended offenders. With that love, they have diverted many from a life of crime. To those volunteers, this book is humbly dedicated.

INTRODUCTION

This book describes what our city courts would be like when Jesus is their inspiration. It is an attempt to relate the life and teachings of Jesus to these courts which have jurisdiction in misdemeanor cases. While there are some exceptions, city courts usually hear and process misdemeanors where the maximum jail term is about 90 days and the maximum fine is usually $500.

The more serious crimes called felonies, many with long prison and even death sentences, are usually tried in state and federal courts.

Why are misdemeanor courts important? First, the vast majority of all crimes are misdemeanors such as fighting (assault and battery), theft, shop lifting, disturbing the peace (loud and profane language often involving intoxication and/or drugs) and most driving offenses.

Second, it is estimated that 70% of all felonies such as murder, rape and armed robbery, are committed by those who <u>first</u> had been convicted of a misdemeanor.

It staggers the imagination to consider what our nation would be like if we greatly decreased the number of those who committed a misdemeanor and, because their lives were transformed by the love of Jesus, did not "graduate" to a life of felonies and prison.

This is the story of how a city court involved Christian volunteers and the love of Jesus to divert misdemeanants from a life of crime to a life of accomplishment and success. It is the story of many misdemeanor courts which have used volunteers from 1959 to 2006.

Since the court is a secular organization, conversion in the tradition of the church to Christianity by confession of faith or baptism is not part of the judicial process. Very often the misdemeanant has never been taught or shown the love of Jesus. By exposing the defendant to this love, he or she becomes aware that Jesus loves everyone – "even me" – a convicted offender.

This city court involved mostly Christian volunteers who were baptized in the faith and who believed in the divinity of Jesus. They believed in the Holy Trinity of God the Father, God the Son (Jesus) and God the Holy Spirit.

There was also another group of volunteers who did not believe that Jesus is God but who lived lives of concern, care and compassion in harmony with the teachings and life of Jesus. These were people of other religions – usually people of the Jewish faith in our country – and secular humanitarians.

This, then, is the story of how a court became a <u>Haven of Hope and Help</u> because its volunteers so lived their lives and shared their lives with the apprehended offender.

When Christians and those living their lives in harmony with Jesus' example and teaching shared their lives with the apprehended misdemeanor offender, the court became more like Jesus would have it be.

Changed by the love of Jesus, they would not become one of the some 70% who first commit a misdemeanor and then a felony and live a life in and out of jail and prison. This is the national estimate most often quoted by criminal justice professionals.

St. Paul tells us we have all sinned and come short of the glory of God. (Romans 3:23) By sharing their lives of successes and failures, of good times and hard times, of victories and defeats, of doing right and doing wrong, the volunteers become the flesh and blood of the words of the court which said, "We want you to live, love and have your being free from crime and failure."

We also recognize that there are religions other than Christianity and Judaism with similar moral and ethical standards. The author is not qualified to write about any religion other than the Judeo-Christian tradition. Thus, for that reason, he has not done so.

FOREWORD

⁓

If Jesus is the inspiration of the court, it would be mission focused on inspiring the defendant to live a changed life by modeling the love of Jesus. It would greatly decrease the vicious cycle of crime by changing the attitude and behavior of the defendant.

Is this effective? Careful independent research verified its effectiveness. There was a reduction of projected subsequent criminal activity of more than 90%. See National Institutes of Mental Health – Royal Oak, Michigan, Municipal Court Research Results, and the comments of Bob Reeves, CPA, in the index.

For Christians, this is not surprising. It is based on court volunteers who love, honor and serve Jesus. It is not a better way, it is the way. They know what Jesus said: "I am the way and the truth and the life;…" John 14:6 (RSV).

I am a retired judge and director of national dissemination of volunteer court organizations who was accepted to attend divinity school but chose law school. Thirty years of intense Sunday School teaching of a high school Sunday School class peaking at over 100 members and a membership in several serious bible study groups for some 25 years followed.

Thus, these pages were authored by a person who, like all of us, sinned and fell short of the glory of God. However, I carefully tried to understand and live the love of Jesus, first taught me by my parents, and I always sought to share that love.

TABLE OF CONTENTS

WHY I
BELIEVE IN
VOLUNTEER COURT MENTORS

"**I** believe in what you are doing (using volunteer court mentors), because nothing else is worth believing in." Honorable Milton G. Rector, retired president of the National Council on Crime and Delinquency, while addressing 1,200 conferees at the Volunteers in Probation, Inc., annual National Forum in Denver, Colorado, in 1973

JESUS, THE ROMAN CENTURION,
A JUDGE AND COURT VOLUNTEER MENTORS

When I was a frustrated, confused and angry young judge with a whole thirty days on the bench, a psychiatrist friend who was far older, wiser and understanding said, "You have to put into the life of the defendants an inspirational personality – a mentor."

He went on to assure me it was our only hope to divert defendants from a life of crime. We needed volunteers who were humble. They needed to know it would be a slow and trying process. They needed great faith knowing the defendants would succeed far more frequently than being punished – and only punished (jail and fines).

I thought of the Roman centurion. He was humble…"Lord, I am not worthy to have you come under my roof; but only say the word, and my servant will be healed." Matthew 8:8 (RSV) Then

Jesus marveled and said, "...truly, I say to you, not even in Israel have I found such faith." Matthew 8:10 (RSV) Because of the centurion's great humility and faith, his request for the welfare of another person, his servant, was granted.

I thought of some of the great mentors in my life. All were humble and not authoritarian. All had faith and none sought after the blessing of healing for themselves but for another – namely me. None simply punished me verbally and physically and then left me.

In addition to the greatest mentors in my life, my mother and father, I needed many mentors to help me at crucial times.

The first was Ms. Margaret Brockman, my sixth grade teacher. When they gave safety patrol belts to the most academic deserving boys, I didn't get one. I was devastated and cried bitter tears that night. I went back to school the next day only because my mother and father forced me. I stood in the hall not wanting to go into class with a feeling of utter humiliation and failure.

Ms. Brockman saw me, walked out into the hall and gave me a hug and a safety patrol belt. Then I walked into class ten feet tall.

Later I won an election as president of the Junior Red Cross – an election I am sure my teacher, whom I wanted to marry when I grew up, influenced. She knew how desperately I needed those victories. Decades later they remain among my most important and cherished victories.

Later, as judge, I would visit her class each semester with my robe and talk to her 6th graders. I often told Margaret I would still be in 6th grade but for her. (I assured her it was only a slight exaggeration.)

Then one of the great honors of my life occurred years later when I gave the eulogy at her funeral, all the time fighting back the tears. I still loved her.

The second great mentor was our high school football coach, John French. Beginning my sophomore year I was about 4'-11" tall and weighed some 90 pounds. I had to finally face reality. My dream of being a football player was not to be. I stood in the hall when the big guys, including some of my classmates, flooded the assembly room to get their uniforms. I had tears in my eyes.

Suddenly Coach French walked out of the room with some 90 kids. He came straight to me and said, "Keith, follow me. I want you to be the manager of our team the next three years. That's important because the team is nothing without spirit and you can help give us what we need most – spirit."

I followed him to the front of the room and into what for me was the first step towards success – a high school diploma. I still think I might well have been a high school drop out if it weren't for Coach John French. Pleasing him was the greatest thing in my life in high school.

Then it was John Cochran of DuBois, Pennsylvania. When I was able to complete one year of college before enlisting in the Air Force because of my young age, I went to Albion College.

Finally I had grown – about six inches and 40 pounds – my senior year in high school and the following summer. Finally I could compete athletically with the guys my own age. During that first semester all I did was play sports and attend classes. No study. Life was all about competing in sports any time with any number of guys anywhere.

"Jack" was an all "A" student, pre-med and president of all kinds of student activities and clubs. He was all everything and I was all nothing. During that first semester he coaxed and pleaded with me to study, to no avail. Finally the marks came out. I was flunking out with less than a "C" average.

"Jack," who was an excellent wrestler and much stronger than I, asked me to room with him. What an honor! It was like a little leaguer sharing a locker with Babe Ruth. The first night in the new room "Jack" explained the rules of the room in our co-op house. Everyone in the room had to go to the library every Monday, Tuesday, Wednesday, Thursday, and Friday nights. Anyone who didn't got beat up.

I had three choices. Quit and go home, get beat up every night or go to the library. I did not like any of the alternatives but decided going to the library was the least of the evils. At the end of the semester when I was called to active military duty, I almost made the Dean's good list with a "B" average. I was on my way to graduation from college and law school, thanks to "Jack."

There were others: two buddies in the military service, a fellow student in high school and college, a six man study group in law school, a lawyer friend after a near fatal tractor accident and always, for over 80 years, my parents, wife and family.

Thus it was, when my psychiatrist friend told me our only hope to divert misdemeanants from a life of failure and a life in and out of prison was to insert into their life an inspirational personality – a mentor, I knew what he was talking about.

My knowledge of what we needed to do and how we needed to do it was not academically imparted to me. It was given to me by Margaret Brockman, Coach French, "Jack" Cochran, my parents, my wife and family and several others in my life.

It was taught to me the same way God taught all of us how to live, love and have our being. It was taught us when the word of God, "I love you and want you to love me," became flesh! I could not learn this from His commandments, laws and rules. We are not rules. We learned this when His commandments became flesh in Jesus. We are flesh and blood. We understand and are transformed by flesh and blood – not only by words, rules and commandments.

We needed to find volunteers who, like the Roman centurion, were humble. They needed to know being a court volunteer mentor took time and patience. Rehabilitation would not be accomplished in a few minutes and with a few words. It would take time and perseverance. They would change lives by living and sharing their lives over many hours and days, not only by their words but mostly by their lives.

Second, it would require faith to sustain them in the months and perhaps years of mentoring. Like the Roman centurion, they would need the depth of faith that caused Jesus to marvel in sheer joy.

Third, like the Roman centurion, the concern had to be not for themselves but others. It would be for the law breaker – the probationer – and not for themselves. Like the concern of the centurion was for his slave – not himself.

Perhaps, most of all, to really believe in and mobilize volunteer court mentors, it is very important to understand, live, honor and obey John 1:14, "And the word became flesh and dwelt among us, full of grace and truth; we have beheld his glory, glory as the only son from the father." (RSV)

For Christians, God's redemption process of mankind climaxed when His words became flesh and blood in our lives. We do not fully comprehend words, laws, rules and commandments. We are not words, laws, rules and commandments. We are flesh and blood. We understand flesh and blood. This is the miracle of Christmas.

When the love of volunteers becomes flesh and blood in the lives of probationers, they became law-abiding citizens. Will it be difficult for the mentors to do? Yes, but it will be <u>nothing</u> like Jesus had to go through to show us how much He loves us.

Thank God for volunteer court mentors. They are certainly the best, and probably our only hope.

A CITY COURT JUDGE'S PRAYER

Heavenly Father, help me to listen very, very carefully and make wise decisions. May no innocent person ever be found guilty. May all those who are very carefully judged to be guilty find in this court a <u>Haven of Hope and Help</u>. May all we do focus on our mission to rehabilitate the defendants and to have them become respected and valued members of society.

May I always involve court staff and volunteers who love, honor and serve Jesus. May we all strive to bring the discipline and love of Jesus into the life of each person who comes before this court.

Let me respect the source of the volunteer's faith in honoring and serving the way of Jesus, be it Christianity, Judaism, another religion or secular humanism.

May I always remember that we are <u>all</u> children of God who have sinned and fallen short of His glory.

May I, as best I can, make Jesus the Judge of this court by constantly seeking to "do justice, to love kindness, and to walk humbly with my God."

Amen

TEN COMMAMDMENTS OF A CHRISTIAN CITY COURT JUDGE

1. You shall treat every defendant as a child of God for whom Jesus suffered and died.

2. You shall determine guilt and innocence carefully and without prejudice, malice or bias.

3. When appropriate, every convicted defendant shall be assigned a mentor who loves, honors and serves Jesus by living their faith or by the way they live their lives.

4. Every convicted defendant, when appropriate, will receive medical diagnosis and treatment from a court volunteer medical doctor, dentist, optometrist or other physical health professional without cost, if appropriate.

5. Every convicted defendant, when appropriate, will receive mental health services from a volunteer court psychiatrist, psychologist, or other well-qualified professional, even without cost if necessary.

6. Every convicted defendant, when appropriate, will receive free counseling, education and other necessary services for alcohol and drug problems and addiction.

7. You shall provide appropriate discipline when the defendant is convicted which is designed to teach the defendant there

is a right and wrong, and wrongdoing results in punishment. However, it must be punishment which ends with restoration and rehabilitation.

8. The defendant will receive assistance in finding employment. Perhaps nothing is more destructive to a feeling of self-worth than the inability to be gainfully employed. Few feelings breed crime more than a feeling of self-hate and lack of pride.

9. You will always be humble knowing that we are all offenders. We have all sinned and fallen short of the glory of God. Those of us who are unapprehended offenders must be very humble in the presence of apprehended offenders.

10. You will always recruit, involve, assist and encourage devoted Christians and those whose lives reflect the love of Jesus to help the convicted defendant to live, love and have their being in a way which honors and serves Jesus. May these Ten Commandments always be on your heart and mind.

JUSTICE

Not only must the court do justly but, if it is to change the attitude and behavior of defendants, they must be convinced they have received justice.

> *"Think not that I have come to abolish the law and the Prophets; I have come not to abolish them but to fulfill them." Jesus.* Matthew 5:17 (RSV) (Underlining supplied.)
>
> *"But let justice roll down like waters, and righteousness like an ever flowing stream."* Amos 5:24 (RSV)
>
> *"...and what doth the Lord require of thee, but to do justly, and to love mercy, and to walk humbly with thy God?"* Micah 6:8 (KJV)
>
> *"For I, the Lord, love justice;..."* Isaiah 61:8 (LB)

THE TRIAL

I t is absolutely imperative that everyone associated with the court is convinced that the trial has been completely fair and just. There can be no doubt that the defendant's rights have been given and observed with meticulous care. It is not enough to merely be satisfied that an appeals court will probably uphold the decision.

To really have the moral and religious fervor to be armed with the power of the love of Jesus to change (the court calls it rehabilitate) the defendant, everyone associated with the court must be convinced, to a moral certainty, that the trial has been fair and justice has been done.

However, that is not enough! The defendants have to be convinced that they have been treated fairly and with justice. If the court is to change the defendant's attitude and behavior, it is at least very advantageous and perhaps absolutely mandatory that the defendants know they have been treated fairly and with justice.

Intently striving to have the court do all it can to convince the defendant he/she has been dealt with fairly and with justice is very important. The court has a great advantage and disadvantage in providing a mentoring relationship. A great advantage is being able to initially force the relationship until it becomes one of friendship. The disadvantage is the greater difficulty in the initial acceptance of the relationship by the probationer. Convincing the defendants that they have been treated fairly and with justice is often the first important key in the acceptance of a volunteer court mentor.

Thus, after the trial or during the pre-sentence investigation, if the defendant claimed he/she was not guilty and the court wasn't fair, they were told they could appear again in court and request an adjournment to take a lie detector test. Such a test, not admissible in evidence, would be carefully and fairly administered by independent certified professionals. If the defendant passed the test, he/she would receive a new trial before a different judge in another court.

This offer, whether pursued by the defendant or not, seemed to satisfy the accused that the court was fair and just and the stage was set for the defendant to be rehabilitated by the love of Jesus.

This, of course, was best for the defendant. It was also best for society where jail and fines only protected society for the 90 day jail term. After 90 days, society was almost inevitably threatened even more with crime because jail virtually always makes the defendant even more hostile and dangerous.

The court also has to be <u>very sure</u> that all pleas of guilty are voluntarily and freely given by the defendants, who fully understand their rights and the charge against them.

When attitudes and behavior are changed, society is protected indefinitely from the ravages of crime.

So the courts whose mission is to change (rehabilitate) the defendant by the love of Jesus began by letting "justice roll down like waters, and righteousness like an ever flowing stream." Amos 5:24

PRE-SENTENCE INVESTIGATIONS

After the trial, if the defendant is found guilty, the court must sentence the defendant. If the court is to be successful in the rehabilitation of the defendant, sentencing must be very carefully and thoughtfully done. A very careful pre-sentence investigation is absolutely essential if the defendant's attitude and behavior is to be changed. Only by changing the attitude and behavior of the defendant can the court help meet the challenge of crime in and to a free society.

> *"Judge not, that you will not be judged. For with the judgment you pronounce you will be judged, and the measure you give will be the measure you get."* Matthew 7:1 (RSV)
>
> *"Judge not according to the appearance, but judge righteous judgment."* John 7:24 (KJV)
>
> *"For he shall have judgment without mercy, that hath shown no mercy; and mercy rejoices against judgment."* James 2:13 (RSV)
>
> *"For true and righteous are his judgments..."* Revelation 19:2 (KJV)

THREE WISE VOLUNTEER RETIREES

I f city court (misdemeanor) judges are to honor, love and serve Jesus, they must be very humble. Any idea that you can look at a defendant for a few seconds and know how to sentence him or her after they have pled or been found guilty is very wrong.

Since these courts rarely have adequate pre-sentence investigations (PSI), this service must be developed. Unfortunately, adequate PSI can not be purchased by these courts which have very limited funds. Too often these courts have no PSI at all. Those which do usually have a probation officer spend a very limited amount of time on PSI. Mostly, the defendant fills out a form which gives minimum information and that form is considered very briefly by the probation officer in his recommendation to the court. This is the situation in the most fortunate of these courts.

To overcome this deficiency, the Royal Oak, Michigan court, a court in which the judge, court staff and volunteers tried to honor, love and serve Jesus, turned to volunteers. Since wisdom and experience were the prime requisites for good PSIs, the judge turned to retirees.

Three retired men were recruited to do pre-sentence investigations. All were Christians in their 70s.

The first was Ralph Shepherd. Ralph was one of, if not <u>the</u> most, loving person I ever knew. His face seemed to just say "love." It was like one ear was shaped like an "L," his cheeks were shaped like an "O" and a "V," and his other ear like an "E."

Ralph used to say, "Be slow to judge for we know little about what has been done and nothing about what has been resisted." If anyone ever followed the biblical verse, "Judge not that ye be not judged, for in what manner you judge, it shall be judged unto you," it was Ralph.

Most often defendants were from seventeen to twenty-one but sometimes older, even into their seventies. Usually when they pled guilty or were found guilty, they were referred to Ralph. They would usually walk out of the courtroom with great anger and go see Ralph, a retired superintendent of schools, in his tiny office.

Usually they would rant and rave for 30 to 45 minutes. Ralph liked his pipe and usually he would fumble around trying to light his pipe while the defendant vented his anger verbally or, less often, just sat in silence.

After about 30 minutes Ralph would take his first triumphant puff on his pipe, exhale out of the window, lay down his pipe and let it go out. Then he would say to the defendant, "Let's chat."

How can you be mad at someone you have been venting your anger against for a half hour or longer who then says, with that ever-present twinkle in his eye, "Let's chat?"

Sometimes two hours would go by while he was "chatting" with a defendant. It was not uncommon to hear crying in the room after an hour or more, and we came to know it wasn't Ralph who was crying. Many defendants said later, "Finally, someone listened to me."

Ralph learned nothing and everything. Asked later where the defendant lived, if he had a prior record, where he worked and other such questions, Ralph would not know. If you asked what was troubling the defendant and what we needed to know to help him, Ralph seemed to know nearly everything.

The most important thing defendants learned is that the court tried as best it could to know who they were and how the court might help them.

The next person the defendant saw was Lou Loefert, a retired investigator for a railroad who had been active mostly in labor disputes. Lou was a very crisp investigator and learned all the facts about the defendant such as his or her age, prior record, employment record, etc. Ralph often said with great admiration, "Lou learned more about the defendant than the defendant knew." Like Ralph, Lou filled out a carefully drafted form which gave information needed to sentence the defendant wisely and effectively.

If drinking or drugs were involved or if defendants said that excessive drinking or drugs was a part of their life, they saw the third retiree, Bill H., as he was called in the Alcoholics Anonymous program. Bill was a retired businessman whose alcoholism and use of drugs had been so severe that he was finally placed in an institution and lost most of his legal rights with his wife as his legal guardian. Bill could relate to the alcoholic, pre-alcoholic, user and addicted drug cases as no one else in the court could.

As an example, when a young drinker or drug user would say, "I can drink or leave it alone," Bill would say, "Not only have I heard these words before, I have said them." Then he would tell the defendant how far he went into intoxication and addiction. Coming from Bill, who had been there all the way, the words often really sank in.

Bill also filled out a written form.

As previously indicated, the defendant could have a whole new trial before another judge if he or she successfully passed a lie detector test. Every attempt was made to convince the defendant he or she was being treated fairly. Rehabilitation is very difficult unless the defendant is convinced he or she was dealt with fairly by the court.

Then Ralph, Lou and Bill would meet and discuss the case. If, in their discussion, they thought they would benefit from the help of another volunteer in the court – usually a psychiatrist or psychologist who volunteered his or her time to the court – they would obtain such an interview and opinion.

After all of this had been done, one of them would write their findings and recommendations on one or more pages. All three would then consider the report and appropriate changes would then be made. The judge would receive their recommendation at least seven days before sentencing and, if I had any questions, ask the three to clarify. If any of the four had any questions after that, further inquiry would be made and, if appropriate, the sentencing date would be delayed.

Sentencing was usually in ten days to two weeks and the defendant was free on bond. If he or she was incarcerated pending sentencing, then sentencing would usually be done as soon as possible.

Why all this very careful sentencing? Veteran judges have often said, "Determining guilt is as easy as rolling off a log when compared with sentencing."

When one realizes that an estimated 70% of all felonies (most serious crimes like murder, rape, armed robbery, etc.) are committed by those who first are convicted of a misdemeanor, we know we must sentence wisely so that this defendant will be more likely changed to live a successful life free of crime and tragedy. The kind of life which is more likely to be lived in harmony with the Lord God Almighty.

It all begins with a very careful determination of guilt or innocence and, if guilty, a pre-sentence investigation that is meticulously done as Jesus would have us do.

The mission of the court is to attempt to change the defendant into a successful and law-abiding citizen by experiencing the love of Jesus in and through its volunteers. It began to achieve its goal by way of a very careful trial, pre-sentence investigation and sentencing of the defendant.

THE VOLUNTEER INSPIRATIONAL PERSONALITY,

THE KEY ROLE OF THE VOLUNTEER COURT MENTOR

"And the word became flesh and dwelt among us." John 1:14 (RSV)

"A prophet shall the Lord your God raise up unto you... him shall you hear in all things whatsoever he shall say unto you." Acts 3:22 (KJV)

"To insert into the life of a young offender an inspirational personality (mentor) is not <u>an</u> answer to crime, it is <u>the</u> answer." Honorable George Romney, former Michigan Governor and member of the President's cabinet. Also a favorite quote of many judges.

"And the Word Became Flesh..." John 1:14

For many Christians there is no more exciting and significant chapter in the Bible and no more awesome revelation from God than John 1, "And the word (God) became flesh and lived among us."

For many generations God had revealed himself to His people by His words and commandments through His prophets. However, we are not words. We are not commandments. We may not really understand rules, commandments and laws. We can obey but too often laws do not transform us and change our lives.

Then, in the fullness of his time, God came to earth and lived among us. He ate with us. He walked with us. He laughed and cried with us and ultimately He suffered, bled and died for us. Then we Christians understood what He intended for us, what we are destined for, how we should live and in whom we should believe.

This is how God redeemed the world. He lived on the earth and showed us how to live while in His human form – Jesus. Often the only way we can change (or rehabilitate) the convicted defendant is when our words, "We want you to be a different person and commit crime no more because we love you," become flesh and blood and are shared in the life of an apprehended offender. Many of these are young men and women 17 to 23 years old.

The court must not just say the words; it must have those words become flesh and blood in the life of the defendant.

To live the first chapter of John, to make it become alive, the court must wrap up its love for the defendant not just in a few words spoken from the highest and most elevated seat in the courtroom but in the flesh and blood of a mentor who lives a life which honors Jesus and who will share his life with the defendant.

It has been said, "Don't walk ahead of me – I might lose you. Don't walk behind me, I can't see you. Walk with me, I need you."

A great poet and minister, Edgar A. Guest, said it this way, "I'd rather see a sermon than hear one any day."

"People change people. Human conduct is changed by human contact." They are words of advice from a wise Ohio judge.

The worst advice a young judge can receive is, "Just bawl them out and fine and jail them. That's the best you can do."

The best advice a young judge can hear is, "Put into their life an inspirational personality who will laugh with them, cry with them and be there for them in their failures and successes. Be like a father always remembering that Jesus told us when we pray to begin with 'Our Father.'"

When courts are mission focused and that mission is to do as Jesus would have us do, then we will begin to meet the challenge of crime in and to the free society we love. This can be accomplished best, and very possibly only, by volunteer court mentors and supporting professional volunteers in our misdemeanor (usually city) courts with their very limited budgets.

THE STORY OF

TWELVE MODERN-DAY

DISCIPLES

AND ONE

APOSTLE

**Courts become <u>Havens of Hope and Help</u> when
Christians and others whose lives reflect the
life and teachings of Jesus become court volunteer mentors**

Note: Some of the following case histories have been taken from <u>Misdemeanors and the Miracle of Mentoring</u>, a 117 page paperback book containing thirty-one case histories from different courts. That book is available from the author.

This book tells of some recent experiences in one court. For more case histories from other courts using volunteers nation-wide, please contact the author.

"And whatever you do or say, let it be as a representative of the Lord Jesus, and come with Him into the presence of God the Father to give Him your thanks." Colossians 3:17 (L.B.)

"...yet wisdom is justified by her deeds." Matthew 11:19 (RSV)

"For whoever shall do the will of my Father which is in heaven, the same is my brother, and sister, and mother." Matthew 12:50 (KJV)

"Go out today and preach the gospel and, if you must, use words." St. Francis of Assisi

HERB AND BOB

Seventeen-year-old "Bob" was very much in love with "Yvonne." Early one evening after a quarrel, Bob stomped out of the house, slammed the door, dashed to his car and sped down the street. Many young children were outdoors playing in a residential area on a hot summer night. Bob was stopped and arrested for reckless driving – 50 miles per hour in a 25 mph zone.

After he pled guilty in court he was asked why he had driven so fast jeopardizing the lives of little children. His reply was simply, "I had a quarrel with my girl friend." "What about?" asked the judge. "I don't remember," said Bob.

Because of a quarrel so minor he couldn't even remember what it was about, he had driven so fast the lives of children were endangered. It just didn't make sense.

In addition to a fine, a restricted driving license and driver violation school, Bob was placed on probation and assigned to "Herb" who was a volunteer court mentor. Herb immediately noticed that Bob was very nervous. After just a few meetings Herb discovered the reason.

Yvonne was pregnant, a condition purposely induced. Yvonne could get married. She was 18. But Bob needed his parents' consent because he was just 17. His parents refused and the months were slipping by. Bob and Yvonne were becoming more and more upset at Bob's parents' continuing refusal to consent. Bob and Yvonne both had jobs, had graduated from high school and seemed to be very much in love. With Herb's urging and encouragement, Bob's parents finally agreed and gave their written consent. Herb was the best man at the wedding.

About a year later, after Bob had met with Herb many times (and sometimes Yvonne had joined them), a very distraught Bob came to Herb with a real problem. "My dad is making improper sexual advances to my wife. What should I do?"

Herb thought he knew why Bob was so agitated, but to confirm his suspicions he asked, "Was your father sexually abusive when you were a kid?" "Yes," Bob replied. "To both my sister and me." Herb felt he had every reason to believe Bob, so he wrote a letter to the father, explaining that they needed to meet so he might better understand and help Bob. There were no more problems of that kind after Herb's letter.

The judge pondered Bob's reaction to this situation and compared it with his uncontrolled anger that previously had jeopardized lives. Now months later Bob had sufficient impulse control to ask his friend for advice.

The amazed judge contacted one of the court volunteer psychiatrists and asked for an explanation for the improvement in Bob's behavior. His response: "Bob was an example of a person who, when an impulse enters his mind, an act immediately results. To have the impulse is to do the act. There is no thought between the impulse and the act. One of the best ways to help such a person is to put into his life an inspirational personality, someone who over time he begins to trust. One who, when the impulse arises, would cause the person to wonder 'What would my friend think?' Now he stops and thinks instead of acting blindly and spontaneously. Bob asked his friend who suggested a way to solve the problem. And he listened to his friend. It is the best way to cure a person who is lacking in impulse control.

Bob and Yvonne have had a successful marriage and many years together. Bob became a good father and husband with the encouragement and nurturing of Herb, his court appointed volunteer mentor who became his friend.

The court, of course, is made up of human beings, all of whom have sinned and fallen short of the glory of God. If we say we have no sin, we deceive ourselves, and the truth is not in us." 1 John 1:8 (KJV) Limited by their humanity, nonetheless they did their best to administer justice and mercy as modern day disciples of Jesus. They sought to bring the love and discipline of Jesus to those who were suffering and downcast.

Herb, one of the original eight volunteers, was the volunteer mentor for Bob, the first defendant to be assigned to a mentor. Thus, Herb became like an apostle to our volunteer court program.

1 Thessalonians 5:14 *"And we exhort you, brethren,… help the weak, be patient with them all."* (RSV)

Acts 20:35 *"In all things I have shown you that by so toiling one must help the weak…"* (RSV)

Psalms 10:14 *"…Thou (the Lord) hast been the helper of the fatherless."* (RSV)

Titus 3:14 *"For our people must learn to help all who need their assistance, that their lives will be fruitful."* (LB)

Matthew 12:20 *"A bruised reed shall he not break, and smoking fat shall he not quench, till he send forth judgment unto victory."* (KJV)

(Matthew 12:20 *"He does not crush the weak, or quench the smallest hope; He will end all conflict with His final victory."*) (LB) Parentheses supplied.

MAX AND DENNIS

"Dennis" was a 17 year old high school senior when he committed a serious (and very foolish) felony.

On Halloween, as a prank, he walked up to a car stopped for a red light and hollered to the startled driver, "Give me your wallet." He shoved a toy water gun at the driver who immediately gave Dennis the wallet and quickly drove away.

Dennis was arrested and charged with armed robbery, a serious felony. The toy gun looked very real. At the preliminary hearing in the misdemeanor court, Dennis said he didn't know what to do with the wallet which he gave to the police without looking into it.

Dennis was a fine student and athlete. He really got scared when the driver drove away. The prosecutor, with the consent of the victim, made a motion to reduce the charge to a misdemeanor. He had more faith in the misdemeanor court with its many volunteers who gave up to 12 hours a month of supervision than the felony court where very competent but totally overworked professional probation officers usually could only give about three minutes a month to probationers.

Dennis was assigned to "Max," a court volunteer mentor. Max was a businessman and fine Christian who met with Dennis about six hours a month for two years. Dennis and Max became friends and soon the court volunteer mentor-probationer relationship became one of friendship, as it often does.

Dennis, who apologized profusely to the victim, worked 192 hours on the community service work crew, finished high school and a year of college, paid court costs and finally his case was dismissed with no record.

Because the court had many volunteers like Max, it could provide rehabilitation and discipline which enabled Dennis to <u>earn</u> a dismissal and avoid a felony conviction.

Years later Dennis, now a college graduate, thanked the judge when he casually met Dennis in a restaurant where Dennis was the assistant manager. He was then about ready to receive his Ph.D. in psychology.

Thus, the words, we want you to succeed in life, became flesh in Max, and Dennis became all that he could be and what God intended him to be.

Thanks to many volunteers, the court became a <u>Haven of Hope and Help</u>. Thus the court did not "crush the weak or quench the smallest hope; and ended all conflict with final victory." The court volunteer mentor, Max, did as Jesus commanded in quoting the prophet Isaiah in Matthew 12:18-20.

> *"...Let the greatest among you become as the youngest, and the leader as one who serves."* Luke 22:26 (RSV)
>
> *"So two good things happen as a result of your gifts – those in need are helped, and they overflow with thanks to God...for this is proof that your deeds are as good as your doctrine."* 2 Corinthians 9:11-13 (The Living Bible paraphrased)

St. Paul tells us that both the giver and the receiver of good works are blessed as a result of the gift from the Christian to the person in need, the apprehended offender. This is what happens when the court seeks to honor, serve and love Jesus.

ELMER AND CHUCK

"Elmer," a high school friend of the judge, was a commercial artist who became a volunteer mentor. Whenever possible, the court tried to match the mentor and the defendant by a mutuality of interest. Elmer's interest and involvement in commercial art proved to be an invaluable asset to the court's volunteer mentor program.

"Chuck," a very sullen, hostile and angry seventeen year old young man was interviewed by the pre-sentence retired investigators. He had just pled guilty to Disorderly Conduct – Drunkenness and Loud and Profane Language.

After several hours of interviews prior to sentencing only one positive fact emerged. "I do like to draw a little," he said almost in a hostile manner. This was noted in the report of the pre-sentence investigators, and they asked if anyone with a commercial art background was a mentor.

Along with an assignment to community service for 64 hours and payment of the costs for such a program, the defendant was assigned to Elmer, the commercial artist volunteer mentor. After a few meetings, Elmer asked "Chuck" if he liked to draw. "Yeah, I do draw some," was his reply. Elmer told Chuck about his interest in drawing when he was in high school and how he had gone to art school after graduation and had become a commercial artist, working mostly with automobile manufacturing and sales. It took several more meetings for Elmer to convince Chuck that he really did want to see his drawings, but Chuck finally did produce some of his work. Elmer later related that "they were all drawings of nudes, but I could see there was talent – raw and undeveloped, but talent nevertheless."

At the next meeting Elmer brought in some of his early efforts, and pointed out how some of his stuff was very crude and primitive, but good enough and he was encouraged by his parents to attend art school. His parents paid his tuition. He lived at home, but also got a 20-hour a week job, and eventually graduated from art school. "When I showed Chuck my early drawings, I explained to him how they gradually became better, and I thought he could do the same thing," Elmer explained.

There was a job opening for an apprentice at the commercial art shop where Elmer worked and Chuck was hired. He also enrolled in art school, taking night classes. He continued this pursuit and graduated from art school. During this time, his interest in drinking and hanging around with the boys gradually faded and a young lady entered the picture. Dates with her began to occupy his time, and his life as a commercial artist was developing. A job with another commercial art firm became available, and Chuck applied for it and was hired.

He later married and became the father of two children of whom he was very proud.

Elmer later recalled, "Yeah, the little rascal became a key artist for one of our competitors." But by the way he said it you knew he was prouder of the picture he painted on the life of Chuck than he was of anything he had ever put on canvas.

As St. Paul wrote, two great things happened (2 Corinthians 9:11-13). One to Elmer and one to Chuck. Because the court had some 500 volunteers who lived their lives in harmony with the life and teachings of Jesus, it became a <u>Haven of Hope and Help</u> for Chuck and many other misdemeanants.

Thus, Elmer, the commercial artist, gave great motivation and help to a young teenager who said, "Yeah, I do draw some." And the greatest became the youngest and the leader as one who serves. Luke 22:26.

> *"Be ye therefore merciful, as your Father also is merciful."* Luke 6:36 (KJV)

> *"Not everyone who says to me, 'Lord, Lord,' shall enter the kingdom of heaven, but He who does the will of my Father who is in heaven."* Matthew 7:21 (RSV)

> *"I preached they must repent and turn to God and do works consistent with repentance."* Acts 26:20 (ML)

> *"Whoever heard of someone lighting a lamp and then covering it up to keep it from shining."* Luke 8:16 (L.B.)

St. Paul, in speaking to King Agrippa, tells us that we prove our love of Jesus – repentance – by our deeds. Thus, we know that not only what we believe is important but so are our deeds and actions.

GARY AND JANE

"Jane," who was about 35 years old, was arrested for shoplifting. She appeared in court with her husband and pleaded guilty. It made no sense. Not only did Jane have no need for the inexpensive necklace she put in her purse and removed from the store, but she had ample money to pay for the necklace.

Jane and her husband left the courtroom to see the pre-sentence investigator.

However the court, which had no money to hire any pre-sentence investigator, had "Gary" who volunteered some 20 hours a week to help the judge sentence defendants as wisely as possible. Gary helped the other three retirees with pre-sentence investigations.

"Gary," a retired university professor and devout Christian, was as baffled as Jane and her husband. One fact came out loud and clear, Jane did not want their two young teenage daughters to know what had happened. Nor did her husband.

They talked about three hours with long periods of silence and thinking. Finally Gary, in later explaining to the judge what had happened, suddenly said, "Did you want to embarrass your husband by dragging him into court? You knew he would come to court and be with you, didn't you?" Jane suddenly gasped and a tear came running down her cheek. Her reaction was so spontaneous and graphic that it could hardly have been faked. Jane suddenly realized not only what she had done but why she did it.

After that it all came out. Jane and her husband had argued a few days before and he did something he never did before. He slapped her.

Gary concluded that Jane wanted to get back at him and she could not do it physically so she subconsciously dragged him into court to get her revenge.

At Gary's suggestion, the judge adjourned the case and ordered Jane to attend the court's marriage counseling class of ten weeks for a total of about thirty hours if her husband went voluntarily. It was taught by a minister whose interests led him to specialize in marriage counseling. He even wrote on the subject primarily to help fellow clergy in marriage counseling. The class went for eight weeks, and Jane and her husband voluntarily attended a second eight week session of about thirty hours.

At the end of the six month period of adjournment, costs were assessed and paid. The case was then dismissed.

A few years later the judge saw Jane and her husband walking hand in hand down the street. They told me they were doing fine.

I had reason many times to thank devout Christians like Gary and the marriage counselor. They knew not only their faith but also their deeds were important in the eyes of God the Father, Jesus, the Son and the Holy Spirit.

The last thing Jane said to me standing on the sidewalk a few years later when we casually met was, "And my daughters never did find out."

Thanks in no small way to Gary, the daughters grew up in a home blessed by a strong loving relationship between their mother and father.

Because Gary and the other court volunteers sought to love, honor and serve Jesus, Jane did not simply pay a fine and leave the court with an undetected problem which threatened her marriage and her children.

Gary lived the words of Jesus when He blessed Jane and her husband "He who does the will of my father who is in heaven." Matthew 7:21

Luke 5:12 *"...Lord, if you will, you can make me clean."* (RSV)

Mark 1:40 *"...if you want to, you can make me well again."* (LB)

Romans 1:5 *"through whom we have received grace and apostleship to bring about the obedience of faith for the sake of his name among all the nations."* (RSV) underlining supplied

WAYNE AND JOHN

"Wayne," a volunteer mentor and automobile executive, made this observation.

"A probationer, 'John,' was assigned to my attention. He had been found guilty of malicious injury to personal property and served several days in jail and was placed on two years probation. His record indicated other minor police problems. John lived with his mother and younger sister in an upper apartment in another city. His father had divorced his mother approximately 11 years before. John was quite confused and wandered as he saw fit.

"John had graduated from high school and was working as a stock boy in a grocery store. He was keeping company with an ex-prisoner of one of our state institutions. Upon my first contact with John, I invited him to our Central Office Building for a luncheon appointment. At first he offered excuses to avoid our meeting saying his driver's license had been taken away and he had no way of getting there. But I arranged transportation. I took him to the Executive Dining Room. He had real long hair and was kind of 'hoody' appearing and made several remarks during lunch about the 'rah rah' boys in the dining room. I tried to keep him interested in what we might accomplish if we worked together.

"For the first several months we had lunch on various occasions and he visited our home. After the first month and a half, I noticed a definite change in his conversation. What he used to think of as sissyish, he now thought good manners. He got a brush haircut similar to mine, and I started to notice that many of his mannerisms were imitating mine.

"About this time, I arranged for him to go to the Social Security Department and take an IQ test that indicated mechanical aptitude. My next step was to get in touch with the Tool Association of our metropolitan area, and working with them I was able to obtain an apprenticeship for him. My problem was then how he could get to and from his job and school. I arranged to meet with the Traffic Bureau, and was successful in obtaining a renewal of his driver's license to permit him limited driving to and from school and work. About six months later his driver's license was restored.

"Approximately one and a half years after starting his apprenticeship course, I received a phone call from John. He said he had something important to discuss with me, and he hoped I would not laugh. He indicated that he had a feeling of inferiority around girls because of his big nose. I had previously noted that he did not mix too well around girls and had noticed that his nose was out of proportion. He seemed quite concerned about this as we made arrangements with the head plastic surgeon at a hospital for him to come in for an appointment. The doctor is a personal friend who I first met in church. After discussing this with the doctor, John said he wished to go through with having his nose changed. An operation was performed changing the appearance of his nose. After recuperating, I noticed he had a girl friend, and John began to blossom into a fine citizen.

"John will soon graduate from a 4-year apprenticeship program as a Journeyman Die-maker, and he is earning a good wage. He also has a fine car and inspires his mother and sister. He plans to enroll in a community college in the fall. He confides in me in most major decisions including the possibility of marriage to the fine young lady he is presently courting. John is certainly a reflection of what has been accomplished by a probation department and its volunteers."

Did all this happen only because Wayne loved Jesus and sought to serve Him? Wayne thought so and thanked God his parents had taught him to love, honor and serve Jesus which led him to "the obedience of faith." Romans 1:5

Wayne had met his "leper" and had cured John's face of it's disfiguring nose. Luke 5:12 and Mark 1:40

> *"And behold, they brought him a paralytic, lying on his bed; and when Jesus saw their faith he said to the paralytic, take heart, my son; your sins are forgiven... and he rose and went home."* Matthew 9:2-6 (RSV)
>
> *"And the man was lowered through the opening in the roof...Jesus said 'Thy sins are forgiven'...And he picked up his bed and walked."* Luke 5:18-24 (RSV paraphrased)

It is very significant that Jesus told the paralyzed man his sins had been forgiven. The heavy and paralyzing weight of his sins was suddenly lifted from him and he was no longer paralyzed.

DR. KNOX AND RAY

"Ray," an 18-year-old, was arrested for disorderly conduct – fighting. He pled guilty.

The volunteer retiree pre-sentence investigator who gave full time service to the court found Ray a very willing talker, unlike so many others. What Ray had to say was also quite unique. The words just seemed to flow out of his mouth like water bursting through a broken dam.

Ralph, the 72-year-old retired superintendent of schools of a small school district and a long-time teacher, listened as Ray spilled out these words:

"I had a fight with my roommate. We are homosexuals who live together. I hate the lifestyle, but there is no other way I can live. I am very evil. I have always been bad, and I always will be. I can't live any other way, but I hate it. It utterly disgusts me," exploded Ray in the small room that barely accommodated a desk and two people.

"How do you know you are evil?" asked the startled retiree.

"My father left when I was very young. I remember only one thing he ever told me. He said, 'You are a rotten, evil, stinking kid. You are bad and you always will be.' I'm sure my mother feels the same way."

The retiree sensed that Ray was an unwanted child, born to parents who were in their late forties. "If you don't want to live that way, why do you?" asked the retired volunteer pre-sentence investigator. "I can't even have a girl friend. I'm too evil. I'm too bad. I'm too rotten," replied Ray, spitting out the words in self-hate and condemnation.

The retiree knew he was confronting a rare situation. He spoke to the judge and requested a month's delay to obtain the opinion and recommendation of one of the court's twenty volunteer psychiatrists, "Dr. Knox."

Dr. Knox, a Christian, talked to Ray and then suggested a further delay in sentencing. He wanted to spend some intense time with Ray. He suggested a 30-day stay at the public psychiatric hospital where he was a full-time employee. Ray eagerly accepted the doctor's invitation. Dr. Knox saw Ray every workday for a month, usually for about an hour each time.

Thirty days later Ray appeared in court and said he was ready to be sentenced. The judge said he wanted to talk to Dr. Knox first and asked, "What happened? Ray said he could now live the kind of life he wanted because he was no longer evil. Is this possible?"

Dr. Knox laughed and reminded the judge of the story in the Bible where the paralyzed man was lowered through an opening in the roof to the feet of Jesus. When Jesus said, "Thy sins are forgiven," the manifestations of the man's deeply ingrained guilt and self-hate were immediately overcome and he picked up his stretcher and walked. Luke 5:18-24

Dr. Knox said with a smile, "We can't do it in a few seconds, but sometimes we can convince a patient over a period of time that they are not evil and hopeless. Over a month's time Ray overcame his crippling guilt and self-hate and a way of life he thought was the only lifestyle available to him. Now he is being restored to health and leaving behind this massive, dominating self-hate and very deep guilt. Assign him to an excellent volunteer mentor. He will need all the help he can get. Right now he's on cloud nine and will need to be brought back down to earth gradually. He will have his highs and lows, his laughter and tears, his successes and failures like the rest of us. But with help, he will make it. His biggest battle is over. He is no longer totally immersed in self-hate and guilt."

Dr. Knox's prediction was right. Two years later his superb volunteer court mentor who became his friend suggested Ray should be released from court supervision. His suggestion was granted. But the story didn't end there.

Some six years later I was wearily completing a long docket of cases that had begun at 1:00 PM and had continued until after 6:00 PM. Finally the courtroom was cleared except for a couple and two small children. I was all out of case files, so I asked, "Can I help you?"

They asked for permission to come through the railing up to the bench where the judge sat. Permission granted. Once next to the bench, the young man said, "My name is Ray. I just wanted you to meet my wife and family. And I want to thank you."

Thus Ray, who is a heterosexual, had been released from his overwhelming guilt complex which resulted in a lifestyle he hated and abhorred by a volunteer Christian court psychiatrist.

The one who really should have received their thanks was Dr. Knox. Unfortunately, he had died at an early age and was unable to receive their thanks. But his love and work lives on in the renewed life of Ray and his family.

The court had become a Haven of Hope and Help because two Christian volunteers, Dr. Knox and Ray's volunteer court mentor, honored, loved and served Jesus.

Mark 9:37 *"Whoever receives one such child in my name receives me; and whoever receives me, receives not me but Him who sent me."* (RSV)

Matthew 25:40 *"And the king shall answer and say unto them, Verily I say unto you. In as much as you have done it unto one of the least of these my brethren, ye have done it unto me."* (KJV)

NANCY AND CINDY

"Cindy" was an 18 year old woman who had been caught shoplifting. It was her first offense and the bottle of perfume was recovered by the store.

At the pre-sentence interview it was obvious that Cindy was very sorry for what she had done. At the suggestion of Ralph, the pre-sentencing investigator and retired superintendent of schools, Cindy was placed on probation and assigned to "Nancy," a homemaker who had been employed as a clerk before her first child was born.

Nancy met with Cindy several times and found her to be very unhappy with her appearance. Her teeth were in very poor condition and Nancy spoke in a way that tried to hide her teeth. She seldom smiled and when she did it was nearly always a quick half smile which covered her teeth.

Nancy asked her about her dentist. Cindy said, "I have never been to a dentist. My step-father tells my mother if he ever gets a bill from a dentist for that kid – me – he will beat us both. We have both been beaten enough so I have never been to a dentist. I know my teeth look real bad and I try not to smile and show them. I'm afraid my breath doesn't smell nice, and I know I can't get a job – even bagging groceries."

Nancy asked the court if it had any volunteer dentists. The answer was "yes." Some 15 dentists said they would work with one case at a time even without costs, if appropriate, in order to help a probationer.

Almost a year later Cindy's teeth were sparkling and so was her life. When dismissed from probation she had a job as a cashier in a grocery store and was paying her dentist at least for the cost of the materials. She had a boyfriend, was going to a community college and had a lifetime friend in Nancy.

Twice a week she babysat as a volunteer for a widow across the street so she could go to school and get a better job. She told Nancy, "I guess I better pay back society a little bit."

Isn't this what the court would do if it was focused on its mission and that mission was to honor, love and serve Jesus? In the eyes of many, Cindy may have seemed to be "one of the least of these" but in the eyes of Nancy she was, and is, very precious – a child of God. God loves his children. So do the court volunteer mentors.

Nancy was one of the many who appear in court fatherless since her stepfather was abusive to Nancy and her mother. God commands us to be very loving to the fatherless on at least 33 occasions. (Nelson's Concordance as a Biblical Words Reference Book of the Revised Standard Version [RSV]. The word "orphan" also appears five times.)

There is no commandment of God more carefully fulfilled by court volunteer mentors than caring for and helping the fatherless. Psalms 10:14

Luke 22:27 *"For which is the greater, one who sits at table, or one who serves? It is not the one who sits at table. But I am among you as one who serves."* (RSV)

Mark 10:45 *"For the son of man also came not to be served but to serve, and to give His life as ransom for many."* (RSV)

Luke 6:49 *"But he who hears* (my words) *and does not do them is like a man who built a house on the ground without a foundation..."* (RSV) (parenthesis supplied)

Acts 8:27-39 *"...An eunuch of great authority...had come to Jerusalem to worship...then Philip...preached unto him Jesus...what doth hinder me to be baptized? And Philip said, if thou believest with all thy heart, thou mayest...and he (Philip) baptized him."* (KJV) (parenthesis supplied

DICK AND BRUCE
AND A WRIT OF REPLEVIN

"Bruce" was a 20-year-old who had not been married very long. He and his even younger wife had a baby.

Bruce got into an argument at work and hit a fellow employee while they were in the parking lot. He was charged with "Disorderly Person – Fighting."

As a first offender, the case was adjourned for two years. The terms of adjournment included 64 hours of community service and payment of the costs of supervision. He was assigned to meet monthly with a volunteer court supervisor and weekly with a volunteer mentor.

Their first three months of approximately 12 hours of meetings were unproductive. But then, one evening the volunteer, "Dick," told Bruce that if he could ever help him in any way to let him know. Bruce sneered and said, "Big deal. You wouldn't help me. I'm just a probationer." "Try me," said Dick. With that, Bruce told Dick that he and his family had been evicted from their apartment. "The landlord said we owed some rent. We don't. Here are my receipts. But the landlord is holding our stove for security for the rent he says we still owe. We can't even warm the baby's bottle."

Dick examined the receipts which seemed to be in order. The next day he went to the court and inquired of the retired full-time volunteer administrator, "Do we have any volunteer attorneys who will help when a probationer has a legal problem?"

"Yes, a volunteer attorney is available for advice if a probationer has a legal problem," answered the administrator. Dick explained the situation and he was referred to one of the volunteer attorneys.

The attorney was convinced Bruce was telling the truth when he examined the homemade lease and the receipts. Then he told Dick, "We need a writ of replevin. I studied replevin in law school but have not had an occasion to use it. Few lawyers do."

Dick responded with "Good, I'll go get one."

"Not so fast," the lawyer responded. "It's a little complicated. I'll have to draw up some papers and go to the court with you. We even need to file a small bond."

The next day the lawyer, Dick and Bruce went to the court in another city and got a writ of replevin. Then they drove to the apartment, and a police officer followed in his car. They served the writ on the startled owner of the apartment. Then the attorney, Dick and Bruce carried the stove out of the apartment and loaded it on the old truck Dick used for hunting and fishing. They drove to the new apartment, carried it into the kitchen, plugged it in – and it worked!

At their next session Bruce told Dick, "I never knew that if you went about something the right way, people – even the police and court – will help you." Needless to say, Bruce was deeply affected by this experience. He finished his period of adjournment without a blemish on his record and became a good husband, father, employee and citizen. Years later he became a volunteer mentor in the court where he was once a probationer.

Bruce was astounded and never returned to court again as a defendant. The courthouse, which in Bruce's mind had always been a monster ready to pounce on him if he did wrong, became a <u>Haven of Hope and Help</u>.

Bruce would not be one of those misdemeanants who would commit some 70% of our future felonies because he found the love of Jesus in the halls of justice. Dick, a Christian motivated by the life and love of Jesus, looked after the weak in our society in their distress.

Isn't this what Jesus would do? Should we not, to the best of our ability, do what Jesus would do if He were the volunteer court mentor? For did not Jesus say he who serves others is greater than he who is served? Luke 22:27

In his 20 years, Bruce had not experienced or learned about the love of Jesus in a church. He was a Protestant only in the sense that he was not a Catholic. In cases like Bruce and too many others, the court learned a great lesson from Philip and the eunuch. Acts 8:27-39

Perhaps the city court, saturated with mission-focused Christians and those living lives in harmony with the teachings and life of Jesus based on other religions and secular values, can successfully help some defendants to live their lives in harmony with Christian values. At least initially this could be more successful than the church in reaching young misdemeanants.

In the story of Philip and the eunuch, a very important eunuch who was in charge of all the treasury of the Queen of the Ethiopians traveled many miles to Jerusalem to worship. We know that to worship in the temple, he would first have to take the ceremonial bath. Upon discovering his body had been defiled by castration, he was denied entry into the temple to worship. Upon returning, he met Philip. Philip instructed the eunuch and told him the good news about Jesus.

When Philip and the eunuch, a castrated male, saw a pool of water in the desert, the eunuch asked Philip if he could be baptized. Philip then baptized him. There was no impediment to his baptism by a rule or custom of a religion.

There are defendants whose parents, relatives, friends or sometimes they themselves have been discouraged by the rules and practices of formal religions and have not joined a church. The court has no such impediment.

Also, there are those who have been angered and hurt by a statement or act of a clergy or layperson of a church. The church is made up of people and people are human. We make mistakes both by our acts and by our words. All of us have sinned and fallen short of the love of God, according to St. Paul.

There are times when mission filled Christians and those who live their lives in harmony with the life and teachings of Jesus can, as court volunteers, help defendants live their lives in a way which is far more pleasing to Jesus.

Sometimes it leads the defendant to join a church or synagogue. Other times it paves the way for the defendant to live a successful and productive life, free from the ravages of crime.

Thus, while the court is not a substitute for showing the defendant the love of Jesus, it is far better than no exposure to His love. It is, too often, the defendant's first view of the life changing love and teachings of Jesus.

Dick introduced Bruce to the love of Jesus and Bruce was never the same.

> *"...Father, I have sinned against heaven and before thee and am no longer worthy to be called thy son: make me as one of thy hired servants...but the father said to his servants, bring forth the best robe...and a ring on his hand...for this my son was dead, and is alive again."* Luke 15:18-32 (KJV)
>
> *"For we are His workmanship, created in Christ Jesus for good works, which God prepared beforehand, that we should walk in them."* Ephesians 2:10 (RSV)
>
> *"And he (the thief on the cross) said, 'Jesus, remember me when you come into your kingdom.'"* Luke 23:42 (RSV) (parenthesis supplied)

It is very significant that the thief on the cross called Him "Jesus" in the more recent and accurate Bible translations. Only the thief called Him "Jesus." Everyone else in direct, individual conversation called Him "Lord" or by some other title. Was there a special relationship between Jesus and the downcast and lowly like a thief? We believe there was. God commands us to care for the downcast like the thief.

PETE AND CHARLIE

〜〜〜

"Charlie" was 19 years of age and was very small in stature. However, he seemed to be far more aggressive and belligerent than most of the defendants who appeared in our misdemeanor court. Perhaps being so small – about 5 feet 4 inches tall – made him even more aggressive than most teenagers who appeared in court. Charlie was very much involved in the use of alcohol and drugs and would "pick a fight" with almost anyone, regardless of their size and strength. Charlie pled guilty to stealing a tire. Like many misdemeanors, it did not make any sense. Charlie did not even own a car.

"Pete" was an insurance agent, a volunteer court mentor and a devoted husband, father and Christian. Pete and Charlie met in Pete's office. Once, Charlie brought his girlfriend with him for a meeting. Pete was astounded. She was beautiful and Charlie was very ordinary looking. Charlie was getting no where fast and Pete wondered how long his girlfriend would be attracted to him. (They did eventually part company.)

Then one day after they had been meeting weekly for about four months, Pete learned of a federal program which taught young men how to operate heavy equipment. Pete learned that Charlie qualified and helped him decide to apply. Pete and Charlie filled out the papers and Charlie was accepted for a school in a state some 1,000 miles away.

Pete asked the court for special permission to pay the difference between the bus fare provided by the government to the Federal training program and an airplane ticket. Permission was granted since there was a rule against mentors giving money to probationers. Charlie went to school in style.

Charlie passed the course and came home to a job in heavy equipment. The future looked bright. Charlie was dismissed from probation.

Charlie was a thief. A thief was very special to Jesus and only a thief called Him "Jesus" instead of by a title like "Lord" or "Master." A thief was very special to Jesus – and to Pete.

Also, Pete was unwilling to have his relationship with Charlie be court volunteer mentor and probationer. He was satisfied with no other relationship than friendship. Like the father in the story of the prodigal son, the relationship could only be father and son. He could not be a hired hand and earn his relationship as a son. He could only be a son.

Charlie and Pete could have no other relationship that would satisfy Pete than a friend. He was a friend who changed Charlie's life.

If anyone had ever gone the second mile to help a probationer, it was Pete. Charlie certainly was "the least of these" in the minds of many and Pete gave himself in Christian love to "one of the least of these." Matthew 25:40

This is what Jesus would do if He were a volunteer court mentor. He would transform the court from a feared monster to a <u>Haven of Hope and Help</u> in the mind of Charlie.

Should we not, as God gives us the power to so do, make serving, loving and honoring Jesus the goal of the volunteer court mentor and everyone associated with the court?

Matthew 9:29-30 *"Then He touched their eyes, saying 'according to your faith be it done to you.' And their eyes were opened..."* (KJV)

Matthew 11:4-5 *"...go tell John what you hear and see; the blind receive their sight..."* (RSV)

Mark 8:25 *"Then again He laid his hands upon his eyes, and he looked intently and was restored, and saw everything clearly."* (RSV)

John 9:25 *"One thing I know, that though I was blind, now I see."* (RSV)

Jesus on several occasions gave sight to Bartimaeus and others who were totally blind. This helped demonstrate that He is the Son of God and the Christians' Messiah and Savior.

GEORGE AND TED

꧁

"Ted" was about 30 years old when he was convicted of a misdemeanor. He was one of the ten to twenty percent of the defendants who were not 17 to 21 years of age.

Ted had had a difficult life. A high school drop-out, he had served time in prison as a felon and had previously been convicted of several misdemeanors, all in other courts. He never knew a father.

At the pre-sentence hearing it was apparent that he had an unskilled job; he worked on rubbish removal. However, several things seemed to indicate that Ted was quite intelligent.

Ted paid a fine and was placed on two years probation and assigned to "George," a businessman, as his volunteer mentor. He was also referred to the court's alcohol and drug addiction school taught by a volunteer who was a recovered alcoholic and who had used drugs in the past. George was a devout Christian.

The court did not use jail. If jail had been successful, Ted would have been one of the nicest men in town – he had plenty of county jail – even some time in a state prison.

The meetings with George followed the usual pattern. Ted saw George at his office one night a week for about eight weeks. Ted said little and George, who knew he had to listen and not preach, listened – too often and too long to silence. He found out that silence is a hard thing to listen to, a tough part of mentoring for many court volunteer mentors.

Finally, one night George gave a newspaper article to Ted to read. It was a simple story which George thought was very funny and maybe they could laugh together.

Ted labored over the article and read it very laboriously and slowly. When he finally finished reading it, and his eyes were moist and slightly red, George asked, "Are your eyes okay?"

"Yes," said Ted. "When I was in first grade they lined us up on one side of the room and printed a big E on the other side. Then they said, 'If you can see the E all right, your eyes are okay.' At least that's what I thought they said. I never took any eye test after that." (He probably was absent when the vision test was completed.)

George knew, of course, that what you see at a distance does not mean you can see well up close. It took George four or five more meetings to convince Ted to go see his friend, "Dr. Miller," an optometrist. Finally, they went together when George explained that his friend would see Ted and examine his eyes without cost to him "as a favor to me," his friend George.

The eye examination resulted in the discovery that Ted's vision was very poor up close and Dr. Miller gave Ted an appropriate pair of glasses for reading which a patient had "outgrown."

Ted began to read extensively, and often he and George would read the same newspaper articles and editorials and discuss them.

Ted then decided to "bone up a bit" and take the G.E.D. test at George's urging. When he passed the G.E.D. test with flying colors, he was dismissed from probation at George's suggestion.

Now he and George made the transition the court always hoped and strove for – and usually achieved - from court volunteer probation mentor and probationer to friends. Ted, who was very intelligent, then enrolled in night school and, about six years later, graduated with a degree in engineering. He moved some 1,200 miles away but George continued to get Christmas cards from Ted for many years.

Who can doubt that one day in the final judgment God will look at George and say, "I was blind but now can see – inasmuch as you have done this for the least of these, you have done it unto me."

What did Jesus do when the blind man said he wanted to see? He helped him and the blind man told the unbelieving Pharisees, "I was blind and now I see." John Chapter 9

George said, "I hope in my own way and in my own time I have met my 'Bartimaeus' and was able to hear him say, 'I was blind but now I see.'"

This is what George did to change the court from a feared program of punishment to a <u>Haven of Hope and Help</u> in the eyes and life of Ted. This is what happens when the city court staff and volunteers are mission focused, and that mission is to honor, love and serve Jesus.

"Let your light so shine before men, that they may see your good works and give glory to your Father who is in heaven." Matthew 5:16 (RSV)

"And God has set some in the church,…gifts of…helps" 1 Corinthians 12:28 (KJV)

"Commit thy works unto the Lord, and thy thoughts will be established." Proverbs 16:3 (KJV)

"Religion that is pure and undefiled before God and the Father is this: to visit the orphans and widows in their affliction, (the helpless), *and to keep oneself unstained from the world."* James 1:27 (RSV) (parenthesis supplied)

LOUIS AND ANDY

⌐≈≈⌐

"**A**ndy" was a probationer assigned to "Louis," a volunteer court mentor in a misdemeanor court. Things seemed to be going along pretty well but Louis was apprehensive. He was more afraid of Andy doing a stupid act than a malicious one. An utterly thoughtless act by a reasonably intelligent young 18 year-old had got him in court in the first place, and Louis was afraid it might happen again.

It did. Only this time it was much more serious. Andy and a "friend" stole a car, drove it to another state some 300 miles away and got stopped by the police. Now it was a federal offense, a felony, and Andy was in prison awaiting his arraignment. Andy called home and told a very distraught father and mother what had happened. They were good parents, as far as friends, neighbors and relatives could tell.

The father had gone to court with Andy when he was previously in the misdemeanor court and put on probation. He met Louis, and appreciated him very much. He called Louis and told him what had happened.

An arraignment date was set in federal court and the father asked Louis, an attorney, if he would go with him to court about 300 miles away. Louis said he would go but he could not appear as an attorney. He was not admitted to any bar association except in his home state.

Louis and the father got into the father's car early one evening after work and checked into a motel after midnight in the city where the federal court was located. The next morning they went to the federal Courthouse and asked the secretary if they could talk to the

83

judge. Louis explained that he was an attorney but could not practice in any state but his home state. He was a volunteer court mentor for Andy and wanted to talk to the judge only as a friend of the defendant. The secretary said she could not promise but if they would come back at 1:00 p.m., the judge might talk to them before the afternoon session.

The federal judge did talk to Louis and Andy's father. He was intrigued with the idea of volunteer court mentors. As a federal judge he operated in a beautiful courtroom with virtually unlimited staff and resources as compared to the very lowly misdemeanor courts. He could hardly believe that hundreds of citizens were serving as volunteer mentors and many more, such as medical doctors, psychiatrists, lawyers, and dentists, were volunteering their time to support mentors and make them more effective.

A few minutes later they were all in court. The federal judge expressed his amazement and appreciation for Louis. He told Andy that he had never known of a friend quite like his volunteer court mentor.

He accepted Andy's plea of guilty and assigned him to a federal probation officer back in Andy's hometown.

He asked Louis to promise to see Andy every week during the three-year probation program and the federal probation officer once a month. He ordered Louis to advise him of any failure to report or any crime committed by Andy at once. He concluded, "There is only one thing keeping you out of prison and that is your friend, Louis. If his reports aren't good, into prison you go as a probation violator. You are luckier than you will ever know to have such a friend."

The three, Andy, his father and Louis, drove home that night. Andy completed his probation successfully and never was in any court again. Andy moved some 1,700 miles away, married and had a very successful career.

Then, 30 years later, he finally returned to his boyhood home, looked up Louis and thanked him for all he had done for him.

The words "God loves you and so do I" had become flesh. Louis' flesh in the life of Andy.

Had it not been for Louis, Andy would likely have gone to prison. He might well have been one of the estimated 70% of those who are sent to prison and return to prison on a new felony conviction within five years after serving their first prison term. Thank God for the "Louises" of this world.

To many, Andy was one of the least of these. He was a convicted misdemeanor offender who then committed a felony. Andy gave his time and love to one of the least of these and therefore gave his love to Jesus. Matthew 25:40

Thus Louis, like the rest of the court volunteers, was a saint. A saint is a sinner who keeps trying to love, honor and serve Jesus.

He gave his time and love to Andy so the court could, to the best of its ability, have as its mission to do as Jesus commanded us to do – to love and help "the least of these."

"And you will be dragged before governors and kings…do not be anxious how you are to speak or what you are to say; for what you are to say will be given to you that hour. For it is not you who speak, but the spirit of your Father speaking through you." Matthew 10:18-20 (RSV)

"I must work the works of Him that sent me, while it is day. The night cometh, when no man can work." John 9:4 (KJV)

"My little children, let us not love in word, neither in tongue; but in deed and in truth." 1 John 3:18 (KJV)

MARILYN AND SALLY

"Sally" was a 24-year-old woman who was very husky and strong. She weighed about 180 pounds and stood about 5'-7." She did not have an ounce of fat on her frame. She could have been a football player – perhaps even a middle linebacker.

She appeared in court on a charge of fighting – disorderly conduct. She was the aggressor and was beating up two other women in a bar. The fight was broken up by some men in the bar and soon the police arrived and arrested Sally.

Sally pled guilty to the charge of disorderly conduct. Fortunately, the judge was presiding in a court which, in addition to fines, jail time, and community service, was able to provide intense, intelligent and individualized probation. This court had many mentor volunteers and volunteers from several professions who supported the mentors. Psychologists, psychiatrists, attorneys, medical doctors, optometrists, drug counselors, and employment counselors were some of the professionals who volunteered their time and expertise under court supervision for as much as 12 hours a month.

After paying her fine, Sally was assigned to a retired supervising volunteer administrator as a term of her probation. She met with him in the courthouse once a month. However, the probation counselor on whom the court really relied was a 33-year-old citizen volunteer named "Marilyn."

Marilyn was a college graduate, and a friend of the judge and many mentors. She was a married, fulltime mother with two children, who included court mentoring in her volunteer activities. She intended to return to the work force when her youngest child was out of high school.

Marilyn met once a week with Sally in the early afternoon. Unlike most volunteer mentors, they met in Marilyn's home. Marilyn told her supervising retired volunteer administrator, "We meet while my young sons are in school. I sure do not want them to hear Sally's vulgar and profane language."

They met for different reasons. Sally attended the weekly meetings because she had to. The alternative was a violation of her probation which would result in further discipline and punishment, the maximum being time in jail. Marilyn met Sally because it was a way for her to serve humanity, her community and her God.

At the end of the first month Marilyn reported to the volunteer 70-year-old retired administrator, who was serving under the direction of a state-appointed volunteer probation officer, "The only positive thing I can report is that Sally is making her meetings. There is nothing good beyond that, and I am hearing a lot of awful language. BUT, she is talking."

Another month went by and Marilyn's report this time included a faint hint of optimism. "Sometimes we go over the required hour – sometimes even two hours, but it is all so negative."

During the third month of meetings an inadvertent and spontaneous statement by Marilyn was to have a dramatic and life-changing effect. Marilyn, in the early stage of their meetings, wanted to tell Sally, "If I can ever help you, day or night, just call me. I will help you all I can." Marilyn knew that earlier Sally had not been ready to hear those words, but suddenly they came out of her lips – and not her mind. Now, after some ten meetings and fifteen hours of being together, they had been said. Marilyn later recalled, "Sally looked at me for a moment with a puzzled look on her face. There was a pause and then she recovered and went on with her negative and vulgar tirade."

Just a few nights later Marilyn's phone rang about 2:00 AM. It was Sally. "I have a sick child and I don't know what to do. I don't have a doctor, and I don't even know where the hospital is." (Sally had told Marilyn she was living with a man and they had two young children. They had moved to Marilyn's city about two months before the bar room brawl.) "I will meet you at the hospital emergency room in 20 minutes," said Marilyn, after giving directions.

Marilyn stayed at the hospital with Sally and her child through the night. The emergency room doctor brought physical and emotional relief to Sally and her child, as well as to Marilyn. As they parted around 8:00 a.m., Sally looked at Marilyn and said, "You care. YOU REALLY DO CARE about me and my family."

With the encouragement of the probation department, Sally and Marilyn no longer had regularly scheduled meetings. When they met now, it was as friends, not regularly scheduled, but now and then, just as friends do. The goal of the probation department was exactly that – to have the probationer/court volunteer mentor relationship become one of friendship.

Slowly Sally began to tell Marilyn about her life. She did not know who her father was. Her only memory of her mother was the day she dropped Sally off at an orphanage where she was raised. She had later spent time in a juvenile criminal institution. At age 17 she was a prostitute for a brief time. Then she met an ex-con and moved in with him. They had two children, but the relationship was tenuous at best.

With Marilyn's help, the relationship grew stronger, and about a year later they married and the family became more stable. Marilyn encouraged Sally to develop her faith, and the family found a church home.

About 18 months after her court appearance Sally was dismissed from probation. She requested a few minutes in private with the judge in his office. "I used to think I wanted to be a movie star, with lots of money. I dreamed of a Cadillac car and mink coats. Now all I want to be is a good wife and mother. I want to love my kids and my husband, and I want them to love me. I want to give them a good home. JUST LIKE MARILYN," said Sally with tears in her eyes.

Twenty-five years later Marilyn received her annual Christmas card from Sally, now living many miles away. She is a very successful mother and grandmother with a good family. They are still friends.

So Marilyn, like some 500 other volunteers, enabled the court, as God gave it the power and wisdom, to focus on its mission to be a <u>Haven of Hope and Help</u> and to serve Jesus. Marilyn's spontaneous statement to Sally, "If I can ever help you, day or night, just call me. I will help you all I can," was fulfilling Jesus' words in Matthew 10:18-20. Sally's problems were, to her, governor and king's size (Matthew 10:18). Marilyn was given the right words and time because the court volunteers were focused on its mission to love, honor and serve Jesus.

"For He (God) *will render to every man according to his works: To those who by patience in well doing seek for glory and honor and immortality, He will give eternal life."* Romans 2:6-7 (RSV) (Parenthesis supplied)

"You see that faith was active along with his works, and faith was completed by works." James 2:22 (RSV)

BILL AND LARRY

❧

It was one of the most heartbreaking cases of domestic violence. The wife, "Peggy," told the prosecutor that "Larry" was a good man, husband and father except when he was drunk. In the past he had often beat her while drunk, she explained. She had never said anything because she loved him. But this time it was different. He involved the children. Now she knew she must do something.

They were both about thirty three years old.

He came home drunk about 3:00 a.m. and slammed the door. Then he climbed the stairs, entered their bedroom and dragged her out of bed and down the stairs. He threw her on the living room floor and screamed at her to stay there.

Then he went upstairs and grabbed the three little children – the oldest was nine – and dragged them downstairs. He threw each one in a corner and began to hit his wife. As he hit her, he told the kids, "Watch and see what will happen to you if you cross me."

Peggy told the prosecutor, "I can take it myself but this time it involved the children. They were terrified."

The prosecutor talked to "Bill," the recovered alcoholic businessman, and Bill came up with an idea. "Don't let him just plead guilty. Make him hear what happened."

When Larry appeared in court, he said, "I plead guilty." The judge said he needed to take some testimony to help in sentencing. Larry scowled but said nothing.

Bill knew this was a case for "tough love," punishment that corrects improper behavior and not that inflicts pain for pain's sake.

Peggy was sworn to tell the truth. She told what happened in the solemn and dignified atmosphere of a courtroom – empty but for the judge, court officer, Peggy, Larry and Bill. As Peggy testified, Larry began to cry – softly at first but eventually with no hope of hiding it.

As Bill explained it later, "I know Larry has no idea of what he did. The same thing happened to me when I was drinking heavily. I think just hearing in the solemn and formal atmosphere of a court what he did will make a big difference."

Larry was found guilty and sentenced to pay a fine and serve two years probation with Bill as his volunteer mentor. He was assigned to the court's alcohol and drug addiction school taught by a recovered alcoholic/addict and was ordered to attend the court's weekly group counseling two year program which used many of the ideas and methods of Alcoholics Anonymous. He and Bill became friends and Larry never returned to court. Bill began as a volunteer court authority figure and soon became just Larry's good friend.

Bill had helped the court become a Haven of Hope and Help by living one of his favorite verses, "The only thing that counts is faith expressing itself through love." Galatians 5:6

Because of Bill and many volunteers like him, the court had as its goal to serve, love and honor Jesus.

RESOURCES FOR
THE VOLUNTEER MENTOR

Probably nothing makes the volunteer mentor more effective than helping the probationer with a problem. Thus, when the volunteer mentor can help find a job, assist in a problem of alcoholism, provide medical or dental services or assist in many other problems, it greatly facilitates the mentor in establishing a warm relationship of life-changing friendship. The next few pages describe some of those resources so vital if the court staff and volunteers are to successfully focus on their mission to help the defendant live a productive life, free of the ravages of crime, by loving, honoring and serving Jesus..

The volunteer mentor lives out the message in John 1:14, "And the word became flesh..." This is the most significant and important ingredient of the volunteer court program. However, other resources were also very important in making the court a Haven of Hope and Help. If the court is to truly focus on serving Jesus, the volunteer mentor needs help in many ways.

ALCOHOL AND DRUG INFORMATION SCHOOL

∞

Robert W. Groves, a superb athlete and former high minor league professional baseball player, saw very heavy combat duty as a marine in World War II. Bob became an alcoholic.

After several years of alcoholism, he committed himself to a hospital for alcoholics. He came out, went to the judge and said he wanted to make up for his lost years. He suggested a program of education for alcohol and drug users. Usually there were eight to twelve probationers who attended each eight week program of about three hour sessions.

Bob enlisted the aid of a chemist who spoke to the probationers ordered to attend the class about the chemical effects of alcohol and drugs. Another visitor was a medical doctor who spoke on the medical consequences. A third visitor was a lawyer/part-time judge who spoke on legal problems. Another speaker was a bartender who spoke on all the self-destructive things people do when they drink too much.

On the first night the probationers assigned to the program took a test on alcohol and its effects. On the sixth night they looked at their answers and were astounded by how much they thought they knew was very wrong.

On the seventh night Bob told his painful story of alcoholism. Nearly everyone had tears in their eyes including an oft-time visitor, his friend from high school, the judge. On the eighth night they just talked. Most of them went out for coffee on the last night and Bob usually didn't get home until about 1:00 a.m.

The next day the volunteer probation department would get several calls. "Can Mr. Groves be my probation officer?" What a change from the sullen and very angry group Bob had started out with two months earlier.

Bob came to view his years of alcoholism as time in prison – the prison of alcoholism – which cost him very much in pain and suffering. He often said of those who were alcoholics and those headed in that direction, "For I was...in prison and you visited me." Matthew 25:35-36.

Would not Jesus visit anyone who is in danger of the prison of alcoholism with a loving Christian like Bob?

EMPLOYMENT COUNSELING

A n employment counselor is another very important ingredient
of the supporting cast. Col. Edward Jacobson, retired from
the U.S. Army and then the Michigan Employment and Security
Commission, volunteered as needed which was usually about two
and one half days a week, to help our probationers find jobs.

He would assist them in filling out employment applications,
develop interviewing skills, and give other help in obtaining employment. He also knew employers and the current employment needs
and was often able to immediately place probationers in jobs.

Unemployment is very devastating both financially and in self-
respect, dignity and pride.

Col. Jacobson played a very important role in the rehabilitation of apprehended offenders by helping them get employment.
He knew how often a job is a very essential element in achieving
dignity, pride and self-respect – vital keys in a life free of crime.

The Colonel was very aware that Jesus said we should love our
neighbor as ourselves. The court needed to help the defendant love
himself.

If Jesus is the model of the city court, He would certainly help
the probationers throw off the anchor of self-hate and to love themselves. Obtaining a job is often a vital step in developing self-love.

SPIRITUAL GROWTH

S piritual growth for the probationer must be done without force or coercion. Courts are a secular organization and no force is appropriate. However, individuals associated with the court can, if asked, provide information on churches and their availability.

Thus, when "Susan" and her intended husband, "Ed," came to court and asked me as a judge to marry them, I saw no reason why I could not ask if they would rather be married in a church. So I asked, and Susan said she would like to but she had long ago drifted from her childhood Lutheran church.

The judge knew the Lutheran pastor and told Susan, "I will call him if you want me to do so." Susan looked at Ed with questioning and longing eyes. Ed nodded and the judge called Pastor "Johnson," the Lutheran minister.

An hour later the pastor, Susan and Ed met and talked. A little later Susan told the judge that she and Ed were going to be married in the church. About a year later the pastor said that Susan and Ed were now members of the church and their baby had been baptized in the church.

This happened a number of times whenever the couple decided they did not want a judge to marry them.

Most of the volunteer mentors were Christian and, when asked, would share their faith in Jesus. Only once was an overzealous volunteer removed from his mentor's role when he was very threatening in his evangelism.

When the court was asked if a marriage by a minister or priest was possible, it responded in an informative manner. Virtually every clergy in the area was available if invited by the probationer.

Jewish probationers and those of faiths other than Christian were referred to their spiritual leaders upon request.

Is this not what Jesus would have us do? We sing, "The Church's One Foundation is Jesus Christ her Lord. She is His new creation, by water and the word. From Heaven He came and sought her to be His Holy bride. With His own blood He bought her and for her life He died."

When appropriate, the court could assure the defendant the church or synagogue would welcome them.

ALCOHOL TREATMENT PROGRAM

The court had its own program of alcohol rehabilitation which drew on the knowledge and experience of Alcoholics Anonymous (AA).

The man who eventually headed the program, which met once a week for two hours, was the first person forced to attend the court program. Years ago he had attended AA for several months and had a period of sobriety only "to fall off the wagon." When he pled guilty to intoxication, he was forced to attend the court's program run by a recovered alcoholic who had benefited from AA for many years and was anxious for a court to try an AA type of program where probationers were forced to attend by the court.

The program was very effective and many recovered from the dreaded disease of alcoholism.

One incident stands out. I happened to meet a man on a golf course. I was startled when the man called me "judge."

"How did you know I am a judge?" The man replied that he had been in the court alcoholism program. Then he said, "I just wish I had met you years ago. I was too proud to admit I needed help and would not go to AA. Then I was arrested for drunk driving and you forced me to attend the court program. I would go and say I did only because that damn judge made me. I don't really need it. Thus, I kept my foolish pride and got the help I needed. I just wish I had met you years earlier. I wasted so many years with my foolish pride."

If the court focused on its mission to serve Jesus, it would certainly have a program to help defendants who were suffering from alcoholism. "Be not drunk with wine. Wherein is excess; but be filled with the spirit." Ephesians 5:18

MEDICAL PROGRAM

~~∽∽~~

The physical health of the defendant was of great concern to the court. A number of doctors were available to do free medical examinations and follow-up treatment.

Dr. Robert Byberg, a fine Christian who taught a Sunday School class of over 100 adults in his Baptist Church, was particularly active in this program of providing medical services to probationers.

He was a very sensitive man who had photographs of many children, youth and adults under the glass on top of his desk. He once explained to the judge, "All of these are people who may have died except for surgery I performed on them. Looking at their photographs is a constant source of inspiration for me."

Would the court seeking to follow and serve Jesus provide healing for the probationers? Of course it would. Did not Jesus say to the blind man, "What do you want?" Luke 18:41 (LB)

Thanks to Dr. Byberg and many of his fellow doctors, we constantly heard the doctor's words to probationers, "What do you want?" Then they provided their medical needs just as they would to any patient.

OPTOMETRISTS

There is no group to whom we owe more than the optometrists. Dr. James Roe, a devout Jew, was a key leader in the court's program. Not only was he the court's first optometrist, but he also recruited his fellow doctors to be involved.

One case stands out. A volunteer mentor was assigned to "Patrick." Pat had an eye that did not focus correctly. He looked very deceitful, almost like he was lying all the time. He appeared to be a "crook" and was fulfilling that illusion. He was in court for theft.

His volunteer court mentor noticed this at once and after about 20 hours of just being there and listening, he thought he could ask about the eye. Pat said he could not see anything out of the eye.

The eye, which was doing no good, was actually doing harm by somewhat distorting his vision and ruining his appearance. "Would you like to see an eye doctor?" the mentor asked. The first response was "no" but after a few more meetings Pat agreed to see the doctor when he was assured there would be no cost.

The optometrist confirmed that the eye was worse than no good. It was actually doing harm to Pat's vision and looks. It should come out and an artificial eye replace it. The optometrist explained that he did not do such surgery but he had a doctor friend who did and "he owes me a favor."

His friend agreed to do the surgery if someone could supply the eye. The mentor was a member of the Lions Club which agreed to donate the eye.

The surgery was performed and Pat had three things he did not have before. His appearance was much better – no longer did he look like a "crook." His vision was no longer distorted. He had a friend who would always be there for him – his mentor.

No longer a probationer, we had every reason to believe that Pat would <u>not</u> be one of the 70% of felons who first committed a misdemeanor. And he wasn't.

In his own way and time, the mentor restored Pat's good sight and appearance.

Is this not what the court would do if it sought to be a <u>Haven of Hope and Help</u> by loving, honoring and serving Jesus? Did he not tell his disciples to tell John the Baptist, "...the blind receive their sight..." Matthew 11:5 (RSV)

Did Jesus not say to His disciples to tell John "...the lepers are cleansed..." Luke 7:22 (KJV) Like Pat, they no longer were victims of a disfigured appearance.

OTHER PROFESSIONAL SERVICES

L awyers, psychiatrists, psychologists, dentists and many other professionals were also involved as indicated in several case histories in the section on volunteer mentors (supra). They helped fulfill God's words, "All of you together are the one body of Christ... (including) those who can help others." 1 Corinthians 12:27-28 (parentheses supplied)

The depth of their commitment and involvement always overwhelmed the judge. One example was a time I was in a restaurant having lunch. A man probably about twenty five years old came to my table and introduced himself as a former probationer. He said, "You know, my volunteer (mentor) was great and we still see each other. But the guy who also really helped me was the (volunteer) psychiatrist who helped me out when I was all screwed up. I've been off probation for almost five years and I still see him when I need him. He still won't charge me anything, but I always leave a few bucks with his secretary. I tell him it's to help with his office rent. What a great friend he is to me!"

The professionals are of tremendous help to the probationers and to the court. Only God knows how many felonies they have prevented.

ADMINISTRATION

The court had seven full time volunteer retirees, four of whom administered the probation program with excellence and three who did pre-sentence investigations.

Volunteer programs must have superb administration or they will not attract and retain volunteers. They cannot maintain their programs and personnel simply with a weekly paycheck. They must attract and retain volunteers by having a superb mission with equally superb administration.

One of the four administrators, "Harry" Hassberger was a retired employee of a plumbing company. He was the chief administrator. He seemed to know everything and be everywhere. Another, a retiree from an automobile manufacturer, was his assistant in the overall administration. A third retiree, also from an automobile manufacturer, administered the community service work program. The fourth, a retired businessman, administered all the group programs like the marriage counseling and alcohol and drug information school. They guaranteed that everything was done with excellence and in harmony with the goals of the probation program.

Three other retirees did the pre-sentence investigations as previously described.

Jesus carefully provided excellent administration for his disciples. "And he called to Him the twelve, and began to send them out two by two..." Mark 8:7. He told them what to take and what to do and "they went out and preached that men should repent. And they cast out many demons..." Mark 12-13 (RSV)

Excellence in administration is absolutely critical for a good volunteer program.

Once our volunteer court program asked a professional business consultant to evaluate the court's administration procedures. After analyzing the program he said, "Your administration procedures and practices are as good as any business I have ever consulted and analyzed in thirty years."

The retired administrators made sure everything was done with excellence. Like Jesus, the court administered its volunteer program with exceptional merit.

While judge, I had an unforgettable moment with Harry Hassberger in the hospital. Harry was on his death bed. It was the day before he died. I had often tried to thank Harry for his great contribution to the Haven of Hope and Help. He worked full time to administer the program for many years as a volunteer. However, Harry would always say, "Nuts to you," and he would hurry away. He wanted no thanks.

Then in his final hours, I tried again to thank Harry. As usual, Harry interrupted but this time, with a tear in his eye, he said, "Don't thank me. Let me thank you. When I retired and before I began to work with the court, my life was pretty much a waste. I know my customers received good service and products but so did those who went to our competitors. Really, all I did was make money for myself and my family. I had really done nothing with my life outside of my family.

"Then, when I was nearly 70 years old, I went to the court to work. The years with the court made my life worthwhile. I helped the court do great things for those who had made a mistake. I helped to change their lives from crime and failure and helped them to become law-abiding and productive. My life is a success. I am now ready to meet my maker. Let me thank you."

It makes you wonder who receives the greatest blessing, the probationer or the volunteer.

Thus, the court truly focused on its mission to be a Haven of Hope and Help. It helped solve the problem which resulted in the defendant being arrested and brought to court. The Christians and those volunteers who honor Jesus by the way they live their lives provided every service and resource it needed.

The problems, attitudes and behavior were carefully diagnosed and treated. The defendant did not "graduate" into a life of felonies and prison. The volunteer court mentors, with all the resources they needed, ended the vicious cycle of convicted misdemeanants later committing an estimated 70% of our most serious crimes – felonies.

Isn't this what a court would do if all of its staff and volunteers were focused on its mission to love, honor and serve Jesus by making the court a Haven of Hope and Help?

DISCIPLINE

T he defendant must know there is a right and wrong, and that wrong-doing will be punished. Discipline is an important part of rehabilitation and plays a vital role in any court where Jesus is honored, loved and served.

> *"...for the Lord disciplines him who He loves...it is discipline that you have to endure...what son is there whom his father does not discipline?...for the moment all discipline seems painful...later it yields the peaceful fruit of righteousness to those who have been trained by it."* Hebrews 12:5-11 (RSV)

DISCIPLINE
WITHOUT DESTRUCTION

After the pre-sentence investigation has been concluded, the judge sentences the defendant. Usually there are two parts to the sentencing: discipline and rehabilitation.

Traditionally, discipline is by jail or a fine. Usually in misdemeanor courts it is a maximum of ninety days and a fine of $500.00.

There is one major drawback with fines and jail terms. They both give a criminal record.

One day Dr. Jack Pearlman, a volunteer court psychiatrist and a devout Jew, told the judge when he finally graduated from the university medical school and became a psychiatrist his favorite professor said, "You will be a great psychiatrist if you just don't do any harm." Perhaps there is a lesson in his words. You will be a great judge if you just don't do any harm.

Pondering his words, I thought of what harm I might be doing and soon concluded that every time I assessed a fine or jail term the defendant would get a record that would make it harder to obtain employment, or possibly join the military service in a chosen branch and many other disadvantages. It would also often affect him or her psychologically.

Considering this, an idea evolved in 1964. Why not adjourn the case and let the defendant do much needed community service? It would be offered only to those who had no record, or a very minor record, and who welcomed a chance to maintain their good record. Only those who were repentant and concerned about maintaining a good record would apply since it was the hard way out. Fathers might pay a fine but no father would be shoveling snow, raking leaves in the city parks, washing city vehicles and other such work. Only the defendant worked!

The case would be adjourned for 18 months to two years and if the defendant had no further convictions, did all his or her work and reported as ordered but off the record to the volunteer probation department, then the case would be dismissed with no record. The defendant would also pay for the costs of administering the program, pay court costs and make restitution to the victim.

One problem remained, the work detail/term of adjournment would have to be very well administered. A retired middle management automobile executive was the answer. Leon Smith administered the program with excellence.

It seemed like this was what Jesus would do if He were administering justice in the city court. He would require repentance, restitution and discipline which was followed with complete forgiveness. Thus, when Zacchaeus told Jesus he would pay anyone he had defrauded fourfold, Jesus said, "Salvation has come to this house." Luke 19:8-9 (RSV) The rich young ruler was told to sell all he had, give it to the poor and then follow Jesus. Discipline was required as part of the forgiveness needed to follow Jesus.

This concept worked very well and the idea became widely used and now community service orders are almost as common as jail and fines nationwide.

As the author looks back on what he has attempted to accomplish over the years, nothing is more rewarding than the satisfaction that many young lives which might have slid into failure and crime with a misdemeanor record are today very successful and productive. Included in this group are at least four ministers of large denominations.

Those who already had a substantial record and those who were offered terms of adjournment/work detail and did not choose it were usually given the more traditional two-year probation along with a fine and/or jail term.

The community service program, often referred to as the work detail program, gave birth to some of the greatest moments in the court which intensely focused on its mission to love, honor and serve Jesus.

The defendants would appear in court, the same court they had first appeared in some two years earlier. They had requested the community service alternative since they had no prior record. They were anxious to keep a good record, so helpful in living a successful life.

They had raked leaves in the city parks and washed city cars and their volunteer mentors had long since become their friends. (Those with special physical conditions could choose to work in the library or the hospital.) They often went fishing together a few times, saw a couple of baseball games, and went shopping together in addition to their usual meetings.

Many had completed the court alcohol and drug school, had enrolled in the public school adult education program, received their high school diplomas and been good citizens. The court had become a Haven of Hope and Help and they had responded very well.

At the final court hearing I (the judge) held up an official-looking document. (It was blank, not filled out.) I said, "This is your record. What do you want to do with it?"

The defendant said, "I want to tear it up and throw it away."

I then said, "Go ahead," and handed the paper to the usually seventeen to twenty one year old young man or woman.

The defendant tore up the paper and, with the nodded approval of his volunteer mentor, the retired administrator, the judge and often a parent, threw it in the waste basket.

I then said, "We really don't throw records away, but we wanted you to know that this is the effect of what happened. Your only record in this court is that your case was dismissed. You can honestly say you have never been convicted of a crime in this court."

Then I said, "Did this court do anything for you?"

The defendant usually would start to say "yes" but I interrupted –

"No, this court did not do anything for you. You did it for yourself. You chose the hard way out. It would have been much easier for your dad to pay a fine. But you chose the hard way which is often the best way.

"You can walk out of here with dignity, pride and self-respect. You earned it. You can be proud of who you are and what you have done." Thus, in exactly the same place where they had stood some one and one half to two years before at one of the lowest days of their lives, the defendants now stood with pride, dignity and accomplishment.

Over the years I was judge, I could not remember a single time a "community service" young man or woman came back to court on a new criminal offense.

Would not Jesus be pleased with a court functioning this way? How often he would meet the needs of sinners and say, "Go and sin no more."

The judge, like most of us including judges, had done wrong as a youth. When I was ten years old, I went into a sports store with a nine year old friend. I admired a fishing reel. When we walked a few blocks out of the store my friend handed me the fishing reel I had admired.

I did not know what to do. I accepted it and, not knowing what to do, did nothing. I was guilty of receiving stolen property – a felony. My young friend would probably have been charged only with shop-lifting, a misdemeanor.

Eventually I smashed the fifty cent reel and buried its parts. I was never apprehended. My punishment was self-inflicted. I never forgot what I did.

So when I took the bench I tried to always remember, "Here am I, an unapprehended felon sitting in judgment of those who only committed a misdemeanor. You have every reason to be very, very humble and to give to others what God gave to you – a clean record. Never forget, when you stumble and fall and get up again, it is as if you had never fallen."

Like so many youthful offenders, I earned dignity, pride and self-respect with no misdemeanor record. Only I earned it with years of regret. (It would have been easier to wash city cars and rake leaves in the city park.)

Perhaps it was part of God's plan. When I faced the first time apprehended offender, I quietly remembered that Jesus had given me a clean record. Could I do any less for the misdemeanants who appeared before me?

Of course not, if I was to try to love, honor and serve Jesus.

THE WOMEN'S PROGRAM

〜

I John 4:7-8

"Beloved let us love one another; for love is of God and he who loves is born of God and knows God. He who does not love does not know God, for God is Love."

"The Women's Division of the Probation Department was developed out of need. Women have different needs than men and require a specific understanding in some areas. Our division was made up of women volunteers who worked one-to- one with a probationer. They were women of varied ages and various spiritual affiliations. The underlying characteristic of all the women was a very deep spiritual commitment and a desire to reflect God's love in a caring way towards their individual probationer.

"I saw great results with the women because of the caring, the attention and the helpfulness of the volunteer. We were a spiritually bonded group of women dedicated to doing God's will. Most of our probationers were afraid to trust and to ask for help. Jesus showed our volunteers how to see their inner needs and help them grow in self-esteem.

"We witnessed many miracles, learned from each other and grew closer to God in doing His work. We secured jobs for our defendants, taught them how to dress properly, had classes on makeup application and helped them see that they were worthy and loving persons who could do great things with their lives.

"This was an experience of a lifetime and one none of us will ever forget."

Romans 8:38-39

"For I am sure that neither death, nor life, nor angels, nor principalities, nor things present, nor to come, nor powers, nor height, nor depth, nor anything else in all creation, will be able to separate us from the love of God in Christ Jesus our Lord."

Barbara Kerby, Director of the Women's Division, Retired.

REPENTANCE

The court, of course, looked for repentance or contrition when sentencing the defendant.

When the defendants seemed to be truly sorry for what they did, the court was far more likely to give the defendant an adjournment with community service and an eventual dismissal than when the defendant had no apparent remorse or regret.

How do we determine if the defendants are truly sorry for what has been done or if they are merely being manipulative? In attempting to determine this, I once again thanked God for the retired volunteer pre-sentence investigators. Ralph Sheppard, the retired teacher, school administrator and superintendent of schools, was particularly helpful in our attempts to determine the true feelings of the defendant.

In John 8:1-11, the crowd brought a woman caught in adultery to Jesus. Jesus, of course, knew if her repentance was real or manipulative. Jesus knew perfectly the hearts of every one He encountered.

Knowing she was truly repentant, He said to the woman, "Go and sin no more."

In our court, many times after the defendant repented not only verbally but by completing successfully all the requirements of many months of court supervision and made restitution to the victim, the defendant heard the judge say, "Go and commit crime no more."

This is what Jesus would do. If the court is to be a Haven of Hope and Help, it must do as Jesus would have us do.

RESTITUTION

No one is more important to the court than the victim. Every effort must always be made to restore the victim and compensate them for their loss.

As a vital part of the pre-sentence investigation, every effort is focused on determining the injury or damage done to the victim. They must be restored as fully as possible to their prior condition.

This is important for two reasons. First, of course, victims have every right to be compensated for their loss. It is simply altogether fitting and proper that we do this. It is basic justice.

Second, an important part of the rehabilitation of all defendants is to right their wrong.

As emphasized elsewhere, Hebrews 12:5-11 made it very clear that discipline is essential for spiritual growth and forgiveness. In the final analysis, the person whose forgiveness is most important is oneself.

The defendants need to forgive themselves. A major ingredient in self-forgiveness is to right their wrong. There is probably nothing more important in self-forgiveness than in righting wrongs.

Determining, ordering and enforcing restitution to the victim is a very necessary requirement of probation or other court supervision. To accomplish this very necessary goal and without funds to hire more staff, the court again turned to that rich source of help, retirees.

George Herrick was a retired businessman whose former duties included financial and fiscal responsibilities. He volunteered up to three days a week to administer our restitution division. When the defendant and the victim could not come to an immediate agreement in court as to the amount of damages, they were referred to George.

George met with both and usually the defendant and the victim would agree on the amount of restitution. George would then collect and disburse the payments, keeping careful records. After all the payments were made, the court was advised that restitution had been paid.

If the defendant, the victim, and George could not agree on an amount, the three would appear in court and the court would set the amount of money the defendant must pay as a term of probation.

If the victim so desired, he or she could withdraw the request for restitution through the court probation program and take their claim for damages to the civil courts. I cannot now remember a single time when that happened and restitution, so important to the victim and the defendant, was accomplished.

The victims received justice and the defendants took a major step in repentance and ultimately forgiving themselves, a major ingredient in their rehabilitation.

Thanks again to a court retired volunteer.

CHARACTERISTICS OF

A JUDGE

There are, of course, many qualifications to be a good judge. Among them are to be learned in the law, be a good listener, courageous enough to do the right thing and be one who will carefully consider all the facts.

However, perhaps one quality stands out over all the rest.

The judge must be

<u>HUMBLE</u>

And to be humble is to be "teachable" – willing to learn.

"...and all of you serve each other with humble spirits, for God gives special blessings to those who are humble, but sets Himself against those who are proud." 1 Peter 5:05 (LB)

"...and what doth the Lord require of thee, but to do justly, to love mercy, and to walk humbly with thy God." Micah 6:8 (KJV)

"...God resisteth the proud, but giveth grace unto the humble." James 4:6 (KJV)

Humility is the first important characteristic for a city court judge who is focused on the mission to have the court be a Haven of Hope and Help, so the defendant will never appear in court again.

St. Paul said, "We have all sinned and fallen short of the glory of God." We all have good reason to be humble.

When Peter told Jesus he would never forsake Him, Jesus told Peter he would deny Him (Jesus) three times before the cock crowed. He was taught an unforgettable lesson in humility a few hours later when he heard the rooster crow. He had denied he knew Jesus three times.

We have been taught that good works alone will not atone for our sins lest any man should boast. We have nothing to boast about.

Humility is not the most natural attribute for a judge to possess. Many judges are amazed at the different way the community views them the day after their election as judge.

One judge put it this way. "The day after the election when I was a judge, I was still the dumb kid who flunked high school chemistry. Yet, it seemed like I was seen in a different light. I knew humility was going to be a difficult task.

"When I took office I soon learned that the whole process was not designed to promote humility. I walked into the courtroom and everyone stood up until I was announced and seated. Like the minister, I was the only one with a special robe and, like him, I sat in the highest chair and spoke from the most elevated position.

"People called me 'Your Honor' and did as I said. Like the Roman centurion of old, 'I say go and they go. I say come and they come.' I am like a small god. My words are immediately obeyed without question.

"A man or woman appears before me with the complexities of problems accumulated over seventeen or twenty five or fifty years of life or more, and I 'solve' them in a few seconds by saying fine or jail. I do this minute after minute, hour after hour, day after day for weeks, months, years, decades and sometimes even for a quarter of a century and more.

"Defendants come before me with problems and most of the time I only multiply their problems by taking away what little they have in money, freedom, and often self-respect. They appear with little dignity and pride and I take away much of what little dignity they have.

"Too often judges, court officials, police and city officials become so accustomed to 'get them in, get their money, or put them in jail and get to the next case' that anything else seems impossible."

Perhaps the ultimate of conceit is to believe that problems have been corrected by this process. Rather, citizens often come in with problems. We multiply those problems and they leave, and too many return on another criminal offense on another day.

Is it any wonder they usually leave the court with hatred for the courtroom and the police who brought them there?

It is also important to remember the story of the prodigal son. This parable teaches us many lessons. One lesson for those of us who are church-goers and law-keepers to remember is who was in the right relationship with the father at the end of the parable. It was not the law keeper (older son), but the law breaker (younger son).

Should judges and others who are law keepers learn humility from this parable?

Perhaps the repentant law breaker (defendant) will finally be in a closer relationship with God than the law-keeper. We all need to be humble. The defendant may ultimately be in a closer relationship with God than the law-keeper (judge, court staff and volunteers).

Is there any way the courthouse can become a <u>Haven of Hope and Help</u> rather than a symbol of suffering and sadness?

Only if Jesus inspires the misdemeanor court by having it become as filled with the love of Jesus as imperfect sinners can be.

This story is how a judge who, like all of us sinned and fell short of the glory of God, tried to be as close as I could to presiding in a court which honored, loved and served Jesus. I did this by surrounding myself with hundreds of Christian volunteers and volunteers who were men and women of other religions or no religion at all who lived, loved and had their being as Jesus would have all of us so live. Volunteers, all of whom had sinned and fallen short of the glory of God and who with humility and understanding gave their love to those who had also stumbled and knew failure and pain.

THE ROLE OF A CHRISTIAN JUDGE IN A CITY MISDEMEANOR COURT

A s a judge in a secular city court, I have seen first hand the effectiveness of mentors with defendants and especially youthful offenders usually seventeen to twenty three years of age.

Now in my retirement I am eager to write about the source of my motivation and the motivation of most of the some seven million volunteers in this national program. It is my hope that the love of Jesus, which has had such an overwhelming influence in my life, will be considered by many other courts and individuals in the judicial system.

I have tried to carefully follow the example of Jesus and to also involve volunteers of other religious faiths and secular humanitarians whose lives reflect Christ-like values.

As I pondered many years on how to best fulfill my duties as judge, I always tried to love, honor and serve Jesus. The constant question in my mind was, "What would Jesus do in this position of authority? How would He perform His duties if He were a city court judge?" This book is an attempt to answer these questions, with the help of some scriptural references which have always guided me and some case histories of volunteer mentors who lived their faith. Most of them are Christian but some believe in other religions and some have secular values which reflect the moral and ethical values of Jesus.

All have played an important role in diverting many misdemeanants from a life of crime and failure. All respect and admire each other.

The Christian judge's role, as I see it, is to set the tone and saturate the court with the disciplined love of Jesus. The judge is not a mentor. The judge does not teach a group counseling course. The judge is not an educator.

As one Illinois judge described the process so well, "I don't do any good myself. I just try to create an organization and atmosphere which enables the volunteers to succeed."

The volunteer usually follows the advise of the St. Francis of Assisi who said, "...preach the gospel and, if you must, use words." They share their faith with their lives. Knowing who they are is more important than what they say.

Does the time come when volunteers can verbally share their faith? Most often this comes after the period of court supervision is over and the relationship has become totally and only one of friendship. Then they often verbally share how they live a life of love because of their belief in and love for Jesus or Moses or Lao Tze or Buddha or another great religious leader. Or perhaps it might be because of their admiration for Socrates or Plato or Thoreau.

When the time comes and the former probationer asks, usually in a less direct manner, "What makes you you?" the mentor can reply and hopefully help his friend begin a journey of faith.

What is the role of the Christian judge who loves Jesus? To do all he or she can do to create an atmosphere which is conducive to helping the defendant love, honor and serve Jesus by making the court a Haven of Hope and Help and not a symbol of suffering and sadness.

Under the glass covering my desk in the courtroom was a constant reminder from the prophet Micah, "What does the Lord require of thee but to do justly, to love kindness and to walk humbly with thy God." Micah 6:8

For me, anyway, it is more important to have the Ten Commandments in the judge's heart rather than on a plaque on the courtroom wall.

To be an enabler and a cheerleader is the role of the city court judge.

THE FAILURES

∽≋∽

As noted by Bob Reeves, a C.P.A. and one of our finest volunteer court mentors, the use of volunteer mentors "resulted in a reduction of projected criminal activity of more than 90% from what might have been expected without the use of mentors and other volunteers." (See index)

How about the less than 10%? Thinking of them is devastating. The failure which was most heart breaking and devastating was "Jack."

Jack appeared in our court on a serious misdemeanor of assault and battery. He severely "beat up" another young man. He could have, and perhaps should have been, charged with a felony by the prosecuting attorney.

Jack pled guilty and a very careful pre-sentence investigation while he was in jail because he could not post bond revealed an aggressive personality. The three volunteer pre-sentence investigators requested and received recommendations from both a court volunteer psychiatrist and a volunteer psychologist.

Finally, after some ten to fifteen hours of pre-sentence investigation, it was determined that Jack should be sentenced to a total of thirty days in jail. The jail term was to be followed by intense counseling including both individual and group psychiatric counseling with one of the court's excellent volunteer psychiatrists. He was also assigned to one of our best volunteer mentors.

Things went along well for about a month. The last report from the volunteer psychiatrist who presided over the group psychiatric program was particularly encouraging. He said, "Jack is making progress. He is starting to listen. Unless he is pushed way beyond normal limits in the next few months, he should have much better control of his emotions."

A few nights later Jack was at a drive-in restaurant and was tormented unmercifully by a young man, also about eighteen, who knew of Jack's probation. Jack finally lost control and went after his tormentor. This time he committed a very serious assault. He was charged with a felony.

Jack was convicted in the felony court and sent to prison, the only time we knew of one of our probationers being sent to prison on a violent felony charge. Shortly after he was sent to prison, we heard that Jack got into a fight with an inmate and was killed.

What do you do? You ask yourself a thousand questions over and over again, "What could I have done differently? Jack seemed much closer to controlling himself. Why didn't I ask a volunteer mentor to visit Jack every day he was in custody and begin the relationship while he was in jail those thirty days on a misdemeanor? Why didn't we ask a volunteer psychiatrist to visit Jack during those thirty days? Why? Why? Why?"

Many successes do not drown out the pain of a failure. Knowing that some 70% of all felonies are committed by a person who first was convicted of a misdemeanor and only one out of hundreds of misdemeanants in our court program was later sent to prison because of a felony helps, but does not eliminate the longing to have that one be zero. We knew that the program really did not fail because Jack was not in it very long. As his volunteer mentor said, "If we could only have known Jack for a year and not just for a month."

Yet, "the Lord is...unwilling that any should perish, but all should come to repentance." 3 Peter 9 (ML)

We can never be satisfied with anything until <u>all</u> misdemeanor offenders are rehabilitated and diverted from a life of crime and failure.

EVEN IF IT IS ONLY SAVING MONEY

Since each repeat misdemeanor and felony costs us thousands of dollars, think of what we taxpayers have saved because of misdemeanor and juvenile court volunteers. When one computes the demonstrated number of criminal offenses prevented as evidenced by the research and survey cited in this book, it is in the millions.

Multiplying the many millions of repeat misdemeanors and felonies prevented by the millions of dollars spent on the apprehension, conviction, probation, parole, jail and prison terms of criminal offenders, volunteers have saved us millions and even billions.

One volunteer program alone, Expeditions of North America (ENA), provided excellent volunteer services to thirty-five sixteen year old juveniles in a juvenile corrections institution in the 1970's. The national average most cited by criminal justice experts is that seventy percent (70%) who were incarcerated at age sixteen will be in an adult prison within five years – by the time they are twenty one years old – because of a felony conviction. To the best of their knowledge, only four of the thirty-five in the ENA program were sent to prison in some twenty-five years, not twenty-five in five years.

That one volunteer program alone saved us many millions. If for no other reason than saving money, volunteers must be involved in juvenile and criminal justice.

We can no longer afford the "luxury" of revenge in our juvenile and misdemeanor courts. Citizen volunteers are our best, and very probably only, answer.

While saving huge sums of money by using volunteer mentors and supporting professional volunteers in our misdemeanor and juvenile courts is a very good reason for citizen involvement, it is not the best reason. The best – the ultimate – reason is that this is God's world and it is God's way.

It is not the best way. It is the only way.

DISSEMINATION

⁀⁀

SPREADING THE CONCEPT OF CITY COURTS BECOMING HAVENS OF HOPE AND HELP BY THE INVOLVEMENT OF MANY VOLUNTEERS

"And they went and preached everywhere…" Mark 16:20 (RSV)

In July of 1959, I was elected to serve as a city (misdemeanor) court judge. For a month I presided in a court which heard trials, determined guilt or innocence and then fined and/or jailed the defendant for up to $500 or ninety days. I was assured that this is all I could do. "It has always been done that way."

Totally frustrated, I asked eight of my friends, a psychiatrist, a psychologist, a social worker, two high school counselors and three clergy, to share my desperate and hopeless situation. Defendants appeared in court, were found guilty or pled guilty and were fined and/or jailed. Soon many were apprehended again and the futile process went on and on. Too often they came back to court, this time on a far more serious crime, a felony like murder, rape or armed robbery.

In my anguish, I asked eight of my friends for their ideas and suggestions. All were devout Christians. They convinced me that the only hope was to "put into the life of a convicted offender an inspirational personality." The words, "we care about you and want you to live productive and good lives," had to become flesh.

One, a psychiatrist, said, "To the extent that you put into the life of defendants an inspirational personality, you will succeed. To the extent you don't, you will fail. It is just that simple."

The eight agreed to be volunteer inspirational persons (mentors) in the lives of convicted misdemeanants. In five years they were joined by some 500 other volunteers. The word had become flesh. John 1:14

The concept of using volunteer mentors and supporting professional volunteers in very well administered and managed programs attracted publicity and financial support to disseminate the concept nationwide.

The Board of Christian Social Concerns of the United Methodist Church and a philanthropist, John W. Leslie, were especially important in launching the national dissemination program beginning in 1965.

The "Reader's Digest" and other popular and professional magazines were very helpful in publicity. Thousands of speeches, consultations, national forums and publications followed.

Independent research by the National Institutes of Health in the mid-1960's indicated the "reduction of projected criminal activity of more than 90% from what might have been expected without the use of mentors and other volunteers." See Introduction to <u>Misdemeanors and the Miracle of Mentoring</u> By Bob Reeves, a Volunteer Court Mentor (CPA) following.

A survey with assistance from the Census Bureau identified 5,657,000 volunteers in thousands of courts from 1959 to 1987. A current survey now in 2006 would indicate many more, probably over seven million, 1959 to 2006.

Information on national dissemination and current resources is available from the author. (See Index)

INDEX

JUVENILE AND FELONY COURTS

This book is written by the retired judge of a misdemeanor court. Virtually everything about rehabilitation is equally applicable to courts with juvenile jurisdiction. Many of the courts which have used volunteers very well from 1959 through 2006, are courts which have jurisdiction in juvenile cases.

No attempt has been made to write the story of these courts since the author of these pages has experience only in courts with misdemeanor jurisdiction. Hopefully, the story of volunteers in juvenile courts, 1959 – 2006, will be written by a judge or official of these courts. It is a very exciting story similar to what is written on these pages.

Also, no attempt is made to discuss courts with felony jurisdiction. I have no experience in such courts. A relatively recent movement has begun in felony courts, beginning about 1998. They are called "Problem Solving Courts."

The basic idea, as we understand it, is for felony courts not simply to decide cases and only pronounce punishment (prison and fines), but to solve problems with appropriate treatment, usually in addition to punishment. In this sense, it seems to be similar to the volunteer movement in misdemeanor courts. Those of us involved in court volunteerism are certainly pleased with the concept of Problem Solving Felony Courts and wish the concept all the best in the years to come.

Only by solving problems and changing the attitude and behavior of defendants can courts protect society from the tragedy of crime in and to a free society.

THE VOLUNTEER COURT MOVEMENT 1959 – 2006
AN EVALUATION OF A CERTIFIED PUBLIC ACCOUNTANT (CPA)

S ome seven million Americans have volunteered their time and professional services in misdemeanor and juvenile courts since the earliest known organized program began in earnest in 1959. In 1987, a national survey with the US Census Bureau identified 5,657,000 volunteers active in criminal justice since 1959. A conservative estimate would be seven million, 1959-2005. Psychologists, optometrists, employment counselors, administrators, pre-sentence investigators, alcohol and drug counselors, and other professionals have unselfishly contributed their unique skills at no charge or at deeply discounted rates in appropriate cases.

The overwhelming majority of volunteers, however, have served as mentors, assigned one-on-one by juvenile and misdemeanor courts. Volunteer mentors take a personal interest in the life of the offender, providing friendship, consistency, a listening ear, a positive adult model, and sometimes much more.

The use of volunteer mentors has proven extremely effective, serving both to rehabilitate the offenders before they "graduate" to more serious criminal activity, and by preventing subsequent misdemeanors and felonies that would have likely been committed by offenders who had not been rehabilitated.

A study by the National Institutes of Health compared results from a normally-staffed probation department, to a similar court jurisdiction with an active volunteer program. Offenders supervised by the court with normally staffed probation experienced about 50% of the probationers convicted of subsequent criminal activity during the next five years. These offenders were found responsible for an average of 5.4 subsequent offenses each. (Please see the index for details.)

By contrast, the court using volunteers (including a volunteer mentor for each offender) found only 15% of probationers committing subsequent offenses in the next five years. Moreover, the average number of subsequent offenses was only 1.5 for these probationers.

Together, the use of volunteers resulted in a reduction of projected subsequent criminal activity of <u>more than 90%</u> from what might have been expected without the use of mentors and other volunteers! Use of volunteer mentors in our misdemeanor and juvenile courts are very probably our best strategy for the prevention of repeat offenses and future criminal activity.

Why are misdemeanor and juvenile courts so critical? The vast majority of all crimes and offenses are tried in these courts. While felonies receive more publicity, misdemeanor and juvenile offenses far outnumber felonies. Moreover, it is estimated that as many as 70% of all felonies are committed by persons who first are convicted of a misdemeanor or juvenile offense.

There is no better place to identify and divert a (usually) young apprehended offender from a life punctuated with habitual criminal activity. This is where our great effort must begin if we are to make significant progress to reduce the incidence of crime in our society.

What motivates this informal army of citizens to serve as volunteer mentors? Some attribute the encouragement they received from their own mentors in bygone years. Some credit religious reasons and cite familiar Old and New Testament scripture. Whatever the initial motivation, nearly all claim the benefits to themselves are every bit as rewarding as the benefits to the offenders.

Hopefully this compilation of a few of the stories about the volunteers' experiences and why they were motivated to give their time and caring attention to a probationer will encourage more courts to create similar programs and encourage more volunteers to participate.

To that goal, this book is dedicated.

Robert Reeves, C.P.A.
Volunteer Court Mentor and
Volunteer Court Consultant, 1965-2003

NATIONAL INSTITUTES OF HEALTH STUDY PROVES VOLUNTEERS ARE EFFECTIVE IN A COURT PROBATION PROGRAM

THE TALE OF TWO CITIES

Court Utilizing Volunteers
Similarity:
Jurisdiction: Adult Misdemeanants
Probation Budget: Similar amount
Description of Probation Personnel:
  12 Part-time Professionals
  7 Full-time Retired Administrators
  10 Part-time Retired Administrators
500 Volunteers: Professional, One-to-one,
  Educational, Administrative, Pre-sentence
  and other volunteers

Comparison Court (No Volunteers)
Similar populations,
Jurisdiction: Adult Misdemeanants
Probation Budget: Similar amount
Description of Probation Personnel:
  1 Full-time Probation Officer
  1 Half-time Secretary

Services Rendered Annually: 50,000 hours

  14,000 hours in Administration
  36,000 hours of Direct Service
  (Professional and One-to one)

Services Rendered
Annually: 3,000 hours

  1,600 hours in Administration
  400 hours of Direct Service
  1,000 hours of Secretarial Assistance

Direct Service to Probationer:
  6 to 12 hours per month

Direct Service to Probationer:
  3 minutes per month

Recidivism Rates:

Recidivism Rates:

Study of all defendants placed on
probation
  Period of Study 4.75 years

Study of all defendants placed on
probation
  Period of Study 4.75 years

Total # placed on probation in

Total # placed on probation in 1

1 year: 310

Number with no repeat offenses during next 4.75 years: 264

Number of probationers committing repeat offenses next 4.75 years: 46

Total number of subsequent offenses next 4.75 years: 71

Offenders committing one or more subsequent offenses next 4.75 years: 14.9%

Number of subsequent offenses per total number of probationers next 4.75 years: 0.23

Attitudes significantly improved during 18 month probation period: 73%
Psychological tests administered.

Attitudes significantly regressed during 18 month probation period: 11.7%

year: 223

Number with no repeat offenses during next 4.75 years: 112

Number of probationers committing offenses next 4.75 years: 111

Total number of subsequent offenses next 4.75 years: 603

Offenders committing one or more subsequent offenses next 4.75 years: 49.8%

Number of subsequent offenses per total number of probationers next 4.75 years: 2.70

Attitudes significantly improved during 18 month probation period: 17.8%

Attitudes significantly regressed during 18 month probation period: 48%

RECIDIVISM RATE: GREATLY REDUCED IN COURT USING VOLUNTEERS

REASON: Psychological Testing/Retesting proves attitudes significantly improved in court using volunteers.

A FEW SUGGESTIONS
FOR BEGINNING A VOLUNTEER PROGRAM

Probably the one most important suggestion is to start small with a few (perhaps five to ten) very carefully selected volunteers and one committed judge (if the court has more than one judge). Then expand your program in the way which is best for your community.

Learn from others but begin and implement the program which is best for you and your community. Your program will be best for you. Develop spirit. There is no substitute for feeling good about what you are doing and who you are doing it with in a cause you believe in with all your heart.

These few thoughts have helped sustain court volunteerism in its growth and success 1959 to 2006.

RESOURCES TO ASSIST IN BEGINNING
AND EXPANDING THE USE OF VOLUNTEERS
IN COURTS

1. <u>Misdemeanor Courts, Hope for Crime Weary America</u>, a 90 page book
2. <u>Courts, Crime and Christ</u>, a 99 page book
3. Visit <u>www.courtmentor.org</u>
4. Syllabus suggestions for a one-hour college credit course, <u>Crime, Courts and Christ</u>
5. Volunteers Prevent Three Million Convictions
6. Brief Summary of Presentations to Judges
7. Crime is a Community Responsibility
8. *Reader's Digest* reprints
9. A Church Seminar – five one-hour sessions
10. <u>Misdemeanors and the Miracle of Mentoring</u>, a paperback book
11. Personal Consultations
12. Join our Quarterly e-mail Service

Please write or call:

Keith J. Leenhouts, retired judge
830 Normandy
Royal Oak, Michigan 48073
248/435-5592

"The author of this book is a retired judge who has spent most of his professional career establishing and mentoring volunteer programs for misdemeanor and juvenile courts nation-wide. There have been some seven million volunteer mentors and supporting professional volunteers involved. Independent research has verified their great effectiveness.

His leadership is solid, effective and inspiring.

He is a Christian who is deeply rooted in the gospel of Jesus Christ. He is an alleluia from head to foot. This program he has put together is the living out of the message and teachings of Jesus.

He would add that others than Christians whose lives reflect the disciplined love of Jesus are also involved in our best, perhaps only, hope to meet the challenge of crime in and to a free society."

Reverend Morris Johnson
St. Paul, Minnesota

Printed in the United States
62012LVS00003B/214-312